Simple
Human
Dignity

Simple Human Dignity

My Life, My Wife, Our Story

Arlene Goldberg
as *told to* Vivien Cooper

gatekeeper press
Where Authors are Family
Columbus, Ohio

Simple Human Dignity: My Life, My Wife, Our Story

Published by Gatekeeper Press
2167 Stringtown Rd, Suite 109
Columbus, OH 43123-2989
www.GatekeeperPress.com

The editorial work for this book is entirely the product of the author. Gatekeeper Press did not participate in and is not responsible for any aspect of these elements.

Library of Congress Control Number: 2020944612

ISBN (paperback): 9781662904035
eISBN: 9781662904042

One

During World War II, women had taken jobs that needed to be filled, as able-bodied men went overseas for military duty. Now that the war was over, they faced the question of whether to remain in the work force or return to the kitchen, which was still thought to be their place at that time. In this climate, in New York City, a little girl was born to loving Jewish parents. They had no idea of the part their daughter would play in changing same-sex marriage laws in Florida.

It is 1947, nearly two years after the official end of the war. Harry S. Truman is the President of the United States, and post-war America is undergoing major cultural changes. The first African American news correspondent (Percival Prattis) is allowed into the U.S. House of Representatives and Senate press galleries, and a film named *A Gentleman's Agreement* is released and will win the Academy Award the following year.

The movie stars Gregory Peck whose character is a journalist who moves to New York City for a high-profile magazine assignment. He finds himself posing as a Jewish man in order to investigate antisemitism for the article. Our heroine will also end up spending much of her early life in New York, and hiding the truth about her life and love.

***

I was born on May 6th, 1947 in the Bronx, New York. My mother, Sylvia, was twenty-two, my father, Jack, was twenty-four and I was their firstborn child. (In those days, people tended to marry and start their families in their twenties.)

My maternal grandparents, Libby and Abe, knew that my parents couldn't afford their own apartment, so they took us in. Grandma Libby and Grandpa Abe's apartment was in Hunt's Point, a Bronx neighborhood filled with walk-up apartments. They lived in a two-bedroom apartment on the third floor of a forty-unit building.

Their daughter, my aunt Rhoda, was occupying the second bedroom. When we arrived, Aunt Rhoda was displaced from her room and slept on the couch. Grandma and Grandpa took one of the bedrooms and Mom, Dad and I stayed in the other.

Aunt Rhoda was sixteen years older than I and very sweet to me. She and her teenage friends would take me to the Bronx Zoo and on other outings. I loved the zoo and especially the ponies and the camels. One time while we were at the zoo, I fell and scratched my knee and Aunt Rhoda and her friends fed me ice cream and treated me like a little princess.

Two years after my birth, my younger brother Leslie ("Les") was born. By the time he was two years old, the apartment would become too crowded for all seven of us—our four-person family, as well as Grandma, Grandpa and Aunt Rhoda. We would move out and find our own place. It was a fourth-floor apartment on Vyse Avenue in the Bronx.

My grandmother was Polish, and Grandpa was Russian. Grandma was a very sweet lady with a love for poetry. She cut poems out of The Daily News and glued them into a diary book for safekeeping. I found that diary one day during my teen years when I was at their house, looking through drawers. The diary opened my eyes to a romantic side of my grandmother. This was a revelation to me.

Grandma Libby was a wonderful cook who handmade the most delicious Jewish food. I was especially fond of her kneidels. Grandma's were denser than other matzoh balls. She served them with carrots and sweet potatoes in a heavenly sauce.

Grandma was very submissive to my grandfather, a strong Russian house painter. That submissive side of her was the only side I ever saw. Grandpa never hit my grandmother, but he would chastise her if he saw her speaking to another man, or even a woman. So, Grandma didn't have any friends of her own. When she got older, she left my grandfather on two different occasions—but she always returned to him.

One time I witnessed Grandpa yelling at Grandma in the middle of a big argument. "Knock it off!" I yelled at him.

He was shocked. "Do not yell at me!" he shouted back.

"I'll yell if I want to," I said, defiant. "Now stop yelling at her!"

After our shouting match, it took a while for Grandpa and me to start speaking to each other again.

I never knew my paternal grandparents because my paternal grandfather died just as I was born. As the story goes, they were in business for themselves and so successful and wealthy, they had their own chauffeur.

Unfortunately, Grandpa was an alcoholic and he cheated on my grandmother. Jewish husbands typically are not cheaters but having alcoholism in the picture changed everything. My grandmother had a nervous breakdown over my grandfather's infidelity and ended up in a mental institution. Meanwhile, Grandpa found himself another wife. Sometime after my grandmother was institutionalized, my grandfather drove to a Philadelphia orphanage for Jewish Children and turned over all five of his children.

This is inconceivable to me. I never understood why Grandpa and his new wife wouldn't have kept the children with them. I would love to know the rationale behind it. Sadly, there is no one left to ask.

Of the five children, only one child was adopted out—my father's younger sister who was adopted into a Christian family. My father, his one younger brother, and two older sisters all stayed together in the orphanage. There they would live out their entire childhood lives, each of them leaving only when they turned eighteen and were of age to be released into society as adults.

My parents were wonderful people. Mom was great and Dad was even greater. My father lived to make my mother happy. Having spent his entire childhood in an orphanage without love or affection, he cherished the love of his wife and family. He showed his love more than most people who have the luxury of taking love for granted.

Dad showed his love for us through his actions. He wasn't shown any love or affection growing up and never had anyone saying "I love you" to him. So, he was a bit awkward and aloof when it came to verbal expressions of his love and affection for us.

I would say, "I love you, Daddy! Don't you?"

"Of course I love you!" he would say.

Rather than become embittered over his time in the orphanage, Dad had learned to appreciate every little crumb he was given. When he got to play on the baseball team, he was thrilled. He played catcher and excelled in the game. When the kids were given one scoop of ice cream each week, my dad was elated and savored every bite. Once he had children of his own, he delighted in giving us big soup bowls filled with ice cream.

My father was my favorite person in the entire world. He was as nice as anyone could possibly be and never said even the most innocuous curse word. He didn't have the opportunity to attend college, but he was so inherently smart, he could add big columns of numbers without a calculator. He watched the news every day without fail and was very political. Dad was right in the center in terms of his political views.

I was always very much to the left, politically speaking. As an interesting side note, my father always told me that the ACLU was a communist organization. Only later in life when I was depending on the

ACLU to come through for me did I realize that my dear father had gotten that one wrong.

Mom had dyslexia and had dropped out of high school in order to help earn money for her family. She became a stay-at-home mother and a good person who had many friends and was well liked. Physically, she was about five-foot-four with a lovely figure. She had long, flowing dark hair and looked like a model until later in life when she got chubby. She had blue eyes and the rest of the family had green, like Dad.

Raising children was hard on my mother. Nevertheless, she was a wonderful mom who had inherited Grandma Libby's affectionate nature. We enjoyed a good, harmonious relationship. Everyone has flaws and my parents weren't perfect. But they gave me everything I needed to grow up well, thrive and be happy. I was very lucky.

Unfortunately, my brother did not have it as easy. He was the middle child and was very mischievous. He also had learning disabilities like Mom and needed tutoring and therapy. He never got the help he needed and felt misunderstood, so he was always acting out. He would steal money from our mother's pocketbook, and she would punish him with spankings.

Mom had a bad temper. Whenever she got angry, she bit her fists to keep from hitting us kids. Unfortunately, she couldn't seem to restrain herself when it came to Les.

I was seven years old in 1954 when my sister, Phyllis, was born. I was glad to have a baby sister and welcomed her with open arms. Not long afterward, my parents began to foster babies. My father never forgot what it was like to grow up in an orphanage without the basic love and care that children need. He wanted to be able to offer that to other underprivileged children. So, he suggested that they foster children.

My mother absolutely adored babies, so they decided to foster infants. The first baby my parents brought into our home stayed with us until the child turned eighteen months. My mother didn't like to foster children who were older than a year and a half. When the babies turned eighteen months, she relinquished them and welcomed another infant in their place.

(Later, when I was about fifteen years old, a little girl named Heidi would come to stay with our family for longer than any of the others. She came to us when she was six months old, with an ear infection. My mother took her in—but this time, instead of returning the child when she grew out of infancy, Mom kept her.

Heidi's mother couldn't take care of her due to a nervous breakdown. She was granted only supervised visits with her daughter. Heidi became so enmeshed with our family, she became like the fourth child. The thing was, we only had three bedrooms, so Heidi had to share a room with Phyllis and me. We had wall-to-wall beds in our room, but it was okay with me. I adored Heidi.

Initially, the social worker told my parents that the only way Heidi would be permitted to stay with us was if she could have her own room. But we begged the social worker to let Heidi stay. And, we explained that Phyllis and I were thrilled to have her in our room with us. We wore down the social worker with our pleas until she relented and agreed. She must have realized how much Heidi was wanted by our family.

Mom and Dad raised Heidi as their own. As time went by, my bond with Heidi deepened. At times, I felt like an older sister and at other times, I felt maternal towards her. Sadly, when Heidi turned twelve years old, she got the terrible news that her biological mother had killed herself by jumping out a window. Heidi took the news really hard.

Even before the suicide death of Heidi's biological mother, Mom realized she was in over her head. Heidi was downright brilliant. Mom was barely able to manage raising the rest of us, none of whom were brilliant. Heidi ran circles around her. When Heidi became traumatized over her biological mother's suicide, she started acting out and running around with undesirable boys.

This behavior sent my mother into fits. One day, Mom fell and hit her head while chasing Heidi and trying to get her to behave. It was clear to both of my parents that my mother could no longer handle Heidi.

My father said, "That's it! She's got to go."

So, Mom gave her away.

When Mom began to see Heidi as a bad child, the fact that Heidi was a *foster* child rather than our own flesh and blood suddenly took on a different complexion. Mom must have realized that she wasn't actually obligated to keep Heidi. So, she decided to send her back to Jewish Child Care Association (JCCA).

Heidi had grown up in our home and came to consider us her family. Being sent away right after the death of her bio-mom was a terrible blow. The fact that Mom never gave Heidi a chance to say goodbye to any of us made it even worse. She sent Heidi away to camp and arranged to have a social worker waiting for her at the bus stop upon her return.

When Heidi took the bus home from summer camp on that fateful day, and found the social worker at the bus stop, waiting to take her away, I'm sure she wasn't saying to herself, *Well, I am just their foster child. We are not blood relations.*

It was true, technically, that Heidi was with us as a foster child. But she had been with us since she was six months old. So, she felt like she was being ripped away from her very own family. I can only imagine how traumatic it must have been for Heidi to have her biological mother jump from a four-story building to her death—and then get sent away by our mother a year or two later. The impact of these two traumas happening so close in time must have been devastating for her.

I was already living away from home by the time that Mom sent Heidi away. Mom told me about it right afterwards. I was terribly upset when I heard that she had the social worker meet Heidi at the bus stop.

"You shouldn't have done it that way!" I told Mom. "You should have brought her home and talked to her about it…not just sent her away!"

"I couldn't tell her myself. I just couldn't." Mom was heartbroken and devastated over doing what she felt she had to do. She felt terrible about it, but she didn't feel she had any choice. She could no longer handle Heidi.

I don't remember talking to my dad about the subject. I do know that my mother was the most important person in the world to my father, and he would have gone along with whatever she wanted to do. In fact, as I said, he supported her decision.

Dad was a loving and supportive father, but he simply wasn't around enough to really have much of a hand in raising us. He left that up to our mother. This was not an unusual arrangement for marriages of that era.

Heidi was taken to a group home called Pleasantville in upstate New York. It had some affiliation with the JCCA. Unfortunately, she suffered sexual abuse at the hands of one of the employees at the group home. The person had also sexually abused several other girls who were living there.

Later in life, Heidi told me that she never forgave me for my failure to visit her there. I didn't drive, but I could have easily asked Carol or my parents to take me to see Heidi.

"If you had come to visit me, you would have known I was being abused," she said.

I was in my early twenties and deep into my relationship with Carol at the time. I was so preoccupied, I put Heidi out of my mind and tried not to think about her. Her situation was painful and disturbing. It hurt my heart deeply to think of her being sent away after being raised with us—and to be sent away in such a terrible way. I didn't want to think about what had happened to Heidi, so I didn't.

I didn't reconnect with Heidi until she was sixteen or seventeen. My parents, on the other hand, never lost connection with her. They began visiting her right away at the facility in Pleasantville. I believe they considered her to be one of their kids but felt that they simply couldn't handle her being under their roof.

My sister Phyllis had suffered during the years that Heidi was with us. She didn't get the attention she needed from Mom. Heidi had joined our household when Phyllis was in her pre-teen years, an age when a girl goes through many developmental changes. Mom was busy with Heidi at the very time Phyllis most needed her love and attention.

Being pushed aside so that Mom could focus her attention on Heidi was hard for Phyllis to take. She was a very good girl, and always did what my parents asked of her. It was frustrating for her that these efforts never seemed to pay off. My sister was such a good girl, she never got yelled at by either Mom or Dad—just sort of disregarded. I believe this hurt her deeply.)

Two

In 1954, not quite a decade after the official end of World War II, America finds itself on the brink of another major war. President Eisenhower warns against United States intervention in Vietnam even as he authorizes huge sums of money in military aid to the country. In April of that same year, Senator Joseph McCarthy opens televised hearings investigating whether or not the U.S. Army is sympathetic to Communism. This sets off the era of McCarthyism in which anyone even suspected of being sympathetic to Communism is in danger of losing their job.

The Hollywood Blacklist arises during this time as McCarthyism spills over into the entertainment industry. This leads to many of the country's favorite entertainment industry professionals being denied employment over flimsy claims and accusations of being Communists. Careers are damaged, lives are ruined, and those living in hiding are driven further underground.

This is no time for a young girl to be feeling the first inklings of lesbianism inside of herself. There is only one societally acceptable family structure in 1954. For proof of this, all anyone has to do is turn on the brand-new RCA color television sets, released into the market that same year, and watch the traditional families featured in the sitcoms of the day.

Shows like Father Knows Best, which transitioned from radio to television that same year, is the status quo and it will be followed by

Leave it to Beaver three shorts years later. The acceptance of "alternative lifestyles" is still decades down the line.

In 1960 Arlene enters her early teens. Meanwhile, Senator John F. Kennedy announces his candidacy for democratic presidential nomination. And, women trade their aprons for bunny ears as the first Playboy Club opens in Chicago.

In March, the United States announces that it will send three thousand, five hundred armed troops into Vietnam. A couple of months later, President Eisenhower signs into law the Civil Rights Act of 1960, thus beginning America's long overdue walk towards equality for all.

Later that year, JFK wins the presidential election. On the heels of his win, the U.S. Supreme Court upholds a Federal Court ruling that Louisiana's segregation laws are unconstitutional, and rules that public transit segregation is illegal. The equality train rolls on, but at a very slow pace.

***

I started to become interested in boys. I developed a big crush on my friend Lynette's brother, Billy. I was eleven and he was sixteen—an older man. We dated a little bit, or as much as you can date at such a young age.

As a result of a split-custody agreement between his divorced parents, Billy came into town only for the summers. He possessed an irresistible combination of sophistication, Irishness, and the allure that comes with being an older man. My crush on Billy—conservative, reserved Billy—seemed like it would last forever.

Then, when I was twelve, Mickey came along, wearing his black leather jacket like Fonzi from *Happy Days*. Mickey was a neighborhood boy who dressed like a thug and carried himself like one. Apparently, I preferred the bad-boy type.

Mickey's parents were the supers of a building across the street from where we lived. One day, we got caught kissing in the back courtyard of his building. A woman living upstairs in the building saw us from her window and started screaming down at us in the courtyard. She kept calling me a tramp.

It was a horrible, heartbreaking experience to be called a tramp for simply kissing a boy I liked. I was still very young and being called a tramp left me feeling deeply ashamed. I wondered, *Is kissing really so bad and wrong?*

Shortly after that incident, my family moved again, and I was glad. Now I would have a chance to start fresh in a place where no one knew me and my reputation was untarnished.

Before we moved away, I met a girl named Molly and we became best friends. She was the daughter of immigrants from Germany. From time to time, I had sleepovers at her house. On one of those sleepovers, we spent some time touching each other.

That early experimental intimacy with another female did not leave much of an impression on me one way or another. I did not have a lightbulb moment where I felt, *This is it for me! I definitely want to be with a girl instead of a boy.*

Back in those days, I didn't even know it was an option to be with a girl instead of a boy. As far as I knew, such things were not done. You grew up, met a man and got married. That was the script that people followed.

Molly was equally unfazed by our encounter. Once I moved away, we fell out of touch and reconnected much later in life when she got married. When I finally came out as a lesbian, Molly distanced herself from me.

Out of self-preservation, I developed the capacity to blank people out of my life. (More on my compartmentalization skills later.) That's what I did with Molly. Once she rejected me for being a lesbian, I filed her away in my memory and she ceased to exist for me.

I was thirteen when we moved to a middle-income housing project in the Bronx called Castle Hill. With this move, we finally had air conditioning.

When we moved to the Castle Hill projects, I made a new friend who shared her secret with me: she was a lesbian. I didn't even know what the word meant and had to look it up in the dictionary.

Before meeting her, I had never known anyone who was gay or lesbian. So, it would never have occurred to me to question whether I was anything but straight. Along with every other girl I knew, I liked boys and planned to grow up and one day get married and have a family.

My parents didn't pay much attention to Walter Cronkite or the evening news, and neither did I. Even if we had been a family that regularly watched the evening news, we would not likely have seen much on T.V. back then about LGBTQ+ issues. Such topics were not widely discussed or covered in the media, and they were nowhere on my radar.

I was vaguely aware of the 1969 Stonewall riots where a gay nightclub was raided by the police, and the gays protested. And, of course, I was aware of historic events like the first trip to the moon and the death of John F. Kennedy. I was more interested in popular culture and was riveted by the Beatles' first appearance on *The Ed Sullivan Show*. I also liked watching *Howdy Doody* with his red hair and freckles (just like Molly), and the *Rooti Kazuti* show.

When I wasn't at school, out somewhere with friends, or watching T.V., my favorite pastime was doing jigsaw puzzles. To this day, I find puzzles to be very enjoyable and therapeutic. It would be many years before the puzzle pieces of my own life would come together to form an entirely new picture of myself.

Right around the time we moved to the Castle Hill Projects, I turned thirteen—the age that I would have been bat-mitzvahed if my family had been observant Jews. Grandma Libby followed some Jewish traditions like lighting Shabbat candles and serving chicken for Shabbat dinner on Friday nights. Mom carried on Grandma Libby's traditions. She would have us kids join her in the kitchen while she waved her hands back and forth over the candles and said a prayer—her own prayer, not a traditional Hebrew prayer. (Dad was always working late on Shabbat.)

Mom wanted to "get some Grandma into me" and pass along the Jewish culture. So, she had sent me to Jewish School when we were still living on Vyse Avenue in the South Bronx. Jewish School was located down a flight of stairs in a cellar. As I walked down the stairs, I was greeted by the musty smell of old books—books that were read backwards.

When I was young, Grandpa Abe had taken me with him to shul from time to time. When it was time to get dressed and go with him, I had to choose a dress that covered my legs. As we walked into the synagogue, he would turn toward the men's section and I would take a seat in the women's section. Even though I had to stay in the women's section, away from my grandfather, I took comfort in knowing that he was there with me.

Also while we were living on Vyse Avenue, we had special deli-style brunches on Sundays. Dad would go to the bakery and pick up huge bags of onion rolls, bialys and bagels and bring them home. We couldn't afford whitefish and lox, so Mom would make tuna fish and egg salad, and lay out cucumbers, tomatoes, lettuce and cream cheese.

I didn't mind my family's attempts to instill in me a sense of my own Jewishness. I found Jewish School and my visits to the synagogue strange but interesting. I was fascinated by the backward books with the writings in Hebrew, and the customs—like wearing prayer shawls and shuckling (swaying back and forth) while davening (reciting prayers). It all seemed very theatrical, but I didn't understand what any of it meant.

My parents didn't talk much about G-d and I don't think they knew much about G-d. This was especially true of my father. He didn't have any Jewish customs of his own, having been raised in an orphanage. Even my mother's customs of lighting Shabbat candles on Friday nights and serving traditional chicken for dinner eventually stopped.

Even after Mom stopped making Jewish chicken for Shabbat, she continued to cook delicious meals for us. She made chicken parmesan and hot tuna-and-noodles-with-cheese casserole. Sometimes we had pot cheese or farmer cheese with noodles. To this day, I love all kinds of cheeses, especially cottage cheese.

On the High Holy Days during my teenage years, my friends and I would get all dressed up and go to the synagogue. None of our families had the money to belong. So, we would stand outside during the services and wait for the services to end, just to feel like we belonged to the Jewish community. This bothered me more in retrospect than it did in the moment. It would later leave me with bad feelings about the religion.

Three

By the mid-1960s, American society is in a serious state of flux. From the cultural landscape to the political one, everything is topsy-turvy, and the music of the day reflects this. The smooth tones of crooners on the radio are being replaced by the sounds of early rock 'n' roll and folk music. Free love and freedom of expression are the watch words of the era.

There is a counter-culture revolution and a sexual revolution afoot and the two are intertwined. Social norms and gender norms are being bent and redefined so fast, it is hard to keep up. While the majority of American households are still loosely following the typical mom-and-dad-and-two-and-a-half-kids-and-a-picket-fence structure, the glue is beginning to dissolve.

In 1961, Bob Dylan arrives in New York City, bringing with him a sea change not only in music but in popular culture as a whole. Little by little, America is leaving behind its rigid gender roles of the 1950s and the country's view of women begins to shift. In April, Judy Garland, who will later become the darling of the LGBTQ+ community, performs at Carnegie Hall.

The following month sees the Civil Rights movement facing terrible backlash, including the bombing by the Klan of a Freedom Riders' bus in Alabama, and the arrest of Freedom Riders in Mississippi. In a case of two steps backward and one step forward, the Apollo space *program is launched. The country will get a man on the moon before it ever achieves equality for all.*

***

The orphanage was all my father knew when he married my mother. He had no family model and didn't know anything about raising children. So, he didn't have much of a hand in raising us kids. He left those duties to my mother.

As I said, she wasn't particularly up to the task herself. She did the best she could. Despite having both a learning disability and a child-raising disability, she gave us plenty of love and affection. The love covered a myriad of deficiencies. I credit her loving nature with the fact that all three of us kids turned out to be good people.

Dad's way of participating in child-rearing was to be loving and kind, and listen intently when I spoke. He was quiet by nature and a great listener. This made me love him even more than I already did. (I wasn't the only one, either. He was beloved by everyone.)

Dad worked nights for the post office, sorting letters. He left the apartment at five o'clock, right before the rest of us sat down to dinner. During the day, he slept. He would be awake by the time I got home from school around three o'clock. That was our only time together during the week—the two hours between three o'clock and five. Then it was time for him to leave for work again. I didn't get to see much of him during the week.

He often worked two or three jobs at one time. He would come home from the post office, get some sleep, get up in the morning, and go work a side job. Even in the cold of winter, he would go out and try to sell window signs to businesses. He was also an aide at my high school. He treasured his family and did everything he could to provide for us.

(It wasn't until later in life that I realized we didn't have much money. As a kid, I had no clue. I always felt like I had everything I needed. I had one doll—a male doll named Bobby. It was one of those squishy, huggable rubber dolls with painted-on hair. None of the dolls in those days were anatomically correct.)

Before Dad left for his post office job in the afternoons, I liked to sit at the kitchen table with him while he ate his dinner. I cherished every minute I had with him. We would talk—or, mostly I talked and he listened—and I filled him in on every little detail of my life. One topic that often came up was my brother, Les. He was usually acting up.

Mom had a hard time handling him. She often disciplined him as a means to try to get him to behave. Some of the discipline Mom meted out to my brother was justified and some of it was not. I did my best to stand between Les and my mother and protect him from her. I knew that she would never hit me. I was the good girl.

From the Yankees to the Giants, my father loved sports. He always read the paper from the front to the back, and he paid special attention to the sports page. He never had the time or money to go to a game, but he followed his favorite teams as best he could.

There was a heavy Italian population in The Castle Hill Projects, and a substantial Jewish population, as well. This was due to the fact that the Jews in our old neighborhood had moved to Castle Hill, as well. (That's the way it was done—we all moved together, as a tribe. Later on, our tribe of Jews would all move together once more.)

The hardest thing about living at Castle Hill was the institutional appearance of the buildings. The project was comprised of several nearly identical buildings, varied only by height. It was like living in a maze. I would wander around, trying to figure out which building was ours. I was constantly getting lost.

One day in the spring of 1960 while wandering around, I ran into a group of kids around my age. They became my friends. This was a predominantly non-Jewish crowd of kids. It just worked out that way.

In my crowd of Castle Hill kids, there was Anthony (Italian), Alice (Irish), another Anthony, and a girl named Carol. I was just about to turn thirteen years old when I met Carol. It's hard to believe that a teenage girl who lived in my complex would come to completely color and consume my world.

These kids were sitting in front of the playground on concrete benches, right next to Carol's building. In front of the benches were tables where people sat and played checkers and chess. On the playground was a basketball court, swings, slide ponds and seesaws.

I was excited to have a new group of friends who knew nothing about the bad reputation I had gotten by kissing Mickey before we moved. I was still hurting over that and was so happy to have a clean slate.

Among the kids in my new group of friends, Carol stood out to me. What struck me about her wasn't her beauty so much; there were prettier girls. There was just an indefinable something special about her. She was thin with very curly brown hair, and very nice.

In many ways, Carol and I were complete opposites. She was quiet and reserved. I was outgoing and popular. I was only a little bit reserved in a crowd setting, as I slowly found my bearings. Carol was intelligent and very easy to talk to. Her quiet, reserved nature reminded me of my dad. Until I met Carol, there was no one on earth I loved as much as my father.

Not long after I met my new group of friends, one of the boys in the group became my boyfriend. His name was Charlie and he already had a girlfriend when we first met. When they broke up, he and I started going steady.

Charlie was tall and handsome, with blonde hair. He was very popular like I was, which was important to me at that time. He was also quiet and reserved like Carol. I found this combination very intriguing.

After a period of time, Charlie and I broke up for no particular reason. As early teenagers, we didn't need a big dramatic reason to go steady or break up. You just found yourself interested in someone else. My someone else at that time was a Puerto Rican boy from the group named Otto.

Otto became my steady boyfriend when I was around fourteen years old, and I would continue seeing him until I was eighteen. In those days, nobody except "bad girls" had sex. It was all very G-rated.

I knew that my mother was not happy about me dating Otto. "You're a nice Jewish girl and nice Jewish girls don't go with Puerto Rican boys!"

So, when he bought me a beautiful angora sweater and an ankle bracelet, I had a real dilemma.

One day, Mom saw me wearing my beautiful, fluffy white Angora sweater. "Who bought you that sweater?" she asked.

I remained quiet and didn't answer her.

My silence was all my mother needed in the way of an answer. She knew that the sweater was a gift was from Otto.

"I don't want you wearing that sweater. He's a Puerto Rican boy! You shouldn't be going out with a Puerto Rican boy or accepting gifts from him."

"It's my sweater now, and I'm going to wear it. It doesn't make any difference who gave it to me."

Given that the sweater was only an item of clothing and not something intimate like a piece of jewelry, she didn't press the issue. The ankle bracelet I received from Otto was another story. Mom saw the ankle bracelet when Otto first gave it to me, and she told me to get rid of it.

"I'll *put* it away but I'm not going to *throw* it away!" I said. "I'll put it in a drawer."

My mother no doubt assumed that I did as I was told. She had no idea that, when I left the apartment in the mornings, I had it with me.

Once I was at school, I would go into the girls' bathroom, take off my stockings, and put the anklet on underneath. I also made a tiny hole in my mesh stockings at the ankle. That way, I could reach in and pull it out before I walked in the door after school.

I managed to get away with this routine for quite a while. Then one night, I was babysitting for a family who lived in the same building as we did. Otto came over to keep me company. Knowing Otto was going to be with me, I put on the anklet so he could see me wearing it.

At some point in the evening, he left and went home to bed. A little bit later, I got up off the couch and promptly passed out. When I came to, I called my mother.

"Mom, I passed out! I must be sick or something. When they get home, you'd better come get me. I don't think I should try to walk home." Since we lived in the same building, I would have typically walked home once I was done babysitting.

Before my mother came to get me, I had the presence of mind to remove my ankle bracelet. I hid it in my makeup compact and put my compact in my pants pocket. When I got home, I took the compact from my pocket and put it in the drawer of the nightstand.

The following morning, I was sick in bed. My family was gathered around me, talking about the fact that I had passed out the night before.

My brother, Les, was absentmindedly opening and closing the drawer of my nightstand when suddenly he noticed the compact.

"What's this?" my brother asked, opening the compact and holding up the ankle bracelet for everyone to see.

"I don't know what that is," I lied.

"You know what that is!" my mother said, without missing a beat. "It's your ankle bracelet from Otto."

Having my ankle bracelet hidden in my compact was seen by my mother as a sign that I had been wearing it even after I promised her I wouldn't. This was true, of course.

Mom took the bracelet, went out the door into the hallway, and headed toward the incinerator on our floor.

Even though I was sick in bed, I got up and went after her in my pajamas. I was pleading with her. "You can't do that! It's *my* gift from *my* boyfriend and it's worth money!"

My mother opened the incinerator door and threw my anklet in. She was oblivious to my pleas for her to stop.

I was devastated—and furious with her.

Otto gave me beautiful gifts. In that sense, he was good to me— but he broke my heart repeatedly. He insisted on going and hanging out with the guys when I wanted him to stay and be with me. I knew I shouldn't have been begging anyone to stay with me, but I didn't like it when he continually chose the guys over me.

I would wander around the playground, crying and crying. All the gifts in the world couldn't make up for the heartache. Throughout our time together, I never stopped trying to get him to stay with me. And, he never stopped leaving me to be with the guys. When he would find me crying, he comforted me. That felt good and encouraged my tears to flow even harder.

When I was about eighteen years old and Otto was seventeen, we broke up. I was fed up with the whole situation. We had dated from the time I was fourteen years old—four years. That was a long relationship for a girl as young as I was then. It spanned very formative years. During our time together, I grew and matured a lot.

When I was nineteen, Otto and I would get back together—but we didn't click anymore. In that one year, I had outgrown him. Suddenly, I felt older and wiser. In our time apart, I had graduated from high school, gone to beauty school and been out in the world. I was more worldly than Otto.

I had also changed crowds. I was now spending my time with the crowd that hung out at the basketball courts. Carol had made the change before I did. I would have naturally followed her over to the new crowd but I had stayed put while I was seeing Otto. This group differed from our old crowd in two significant ways: they were mostly Jewish and they were college bound.

College was the furthest thing from my mind. It was free in those days and I could have gone if I wanted to. Oddly, my parents never even brought it up. My mother told me that I was going to grow up and be a secretary. (Ironically, I would end up in professional roles where I *needed* a secretary.)

I didn't argue the point with my parents. We all knew that I hated school, struggled with it and generally did poorly with my studies. History in particular was a subject that was very hard for me. I felt that the school ship had sailed, and I wasn't on it. Carol could have done much better in college but she wasn't planning to go either. Her parents had never presented it as an option to her either.

As we went through our high-school graduation ceremony, she was right behind me. Her last name was Goldwasser and mine is Goldberg. Given that I had done poorly in school, I was grateful to graduate. I often wondered if my dad, a part-time aide at my high school, had pulled strings to make sure I got my diploma.

After graduation, I went through Wilfred Hairdressing Academy, and worked in a salon for a year or so. I quickly realized that it wasn't a good fit for me. First of all, I didn't do as well at the academy as I had hoped. I also found many of the clients to be rude. (One particularly distasteful memory involves a ten-cent tip from a client.)

I left hairdressing behind me and went to work at Korvettes, a department store where Carol had an office job. I worked in the money room, counting the daily receipts from the store. (Korvettes was a precursor to the superstores of today, like Target.)

Four

Suddenly, the rigid structures that defined American life are becoming wobbly. Sex is no longer confined to heterosexual marriage, and gender bending is not only being tolerated but celebrated, as evidenced by the highly lauded work of androgynous artists like Andy Warhol and David Bowie.

The Vietnam War is in full swing, America is involved in a race to the moon, and Aretha Franklin releases her pro-woman anthem that would come to define a generation: R-e-s-p-e-c-t. And in Manhattan, mere miles from where Arlene and her family are living, ten thousand people descend upon Central Park for a be-in, in protest against the Vietnam War and racism.

By the end of the 1960s, women's desire to be taken seriously and treated equally reaches a fever pitch and gains momentum. The Women's Movement is here to stay.

***

For the most part, I was a good girl. I had been raised with very strong ethics. I also grew up with the knowledge that my parents loved me and had complete faith in me. Ironically, their love and faith gave me the strength I needed to defy them at times.

I saw myself as someone who knew right from wrong and would always choose the right path. So, I didn't want anyone—including my own parents, whom I loved dearly—trying to order me around and tell me what to do and what not to do.

If I was out with friends and came home later than the time my parents were expecting me, so what? I knew that I would go home eventually and that I wasn't doing anything so terrible. As long as I could justify my actions as being reasonable, I saw no reason that I needed to obey my parents, explain myself, or necessarily reveal the truth about what I was doing.

There was the time, for example, that I went out drinking with some of my friends down at The End. It was so named because of its location at the end of Castle Hill Avenue by the Hutchinson River. The crowd and I were drinking that night and stayed out too late. We didn't realize that our parents were out looking for us. We didn't know that, when they couldn't find us, they got the police involved.

I did things I felt were right for *me*—not for my parents. I figured that I had earned that right. After all, I accepted and handled the responsibilities entrusted to me every day. There were times, for example, when it was my responsibility to take care of my brother and sister. To a large extent, I was also left in charge of Heidi.

I instinctively rejected anything that felt like a double standard. I thought, *Well, if you think I'm mature enough to handle these things and make good decisions, I must be enough of an adult to handle myself and my own life as I see fit.*

When I had been working at Korvettes for a year or so, Carol took a trip to Florida with two friends of ours, Gloria and Janet. (I couldn't get the time off work to go on the trip.) The four of us were very close and often got together for outings to the beach or the movies. Sometimes the four of us just hung out at Carol's family's place, talking and listening to records. When we were hanging out, Carol liked to lay with her head in my lap.

At the time, I didn't give it a second thought. Then, very slowly over time, our relationship began to shift. There was something different about our conversations and the way she looked at me. Before I knew what had happened, we became very close.

In the evenings, we were often out with the crowd at the basketball courts. When we got in after spending an evening together, we liked to have sleepovers. Sometimes I would sleep at her place and sometimes she would sleep at mine. When I slept over at Carol's, I took her sister's bed and she had to sleep in the living room. (They shared a bedroom.)

It was a beautiful, carefree time of life and each amazing day seemed to last forever. I loved every minute of it. I had a big circle of friends, was very popular, and had a fulfilling social life. When we weren't hanging out with the crowd, both Carol and I acted in plays at the YMCA and YWCA community centers. On the home front, things were also going smoothly and life was wonderful there too.

(I took those times for granted to some extent, which is a luxury afforded to the young. These days, I cherish every single minute of my life. I'll never forget my mother saying to me repeatedly, "I'm old! I'm old!" She was only thirty at the time. I never want to feel like I am too old to enjoy my life.)

When we were both twenty years old, Carol and I spent the evening hanging out at the basketball courts with the usual crowd. We decided to sleep at her place that evening. When we got there, her family was still up. We sat with them for a while, watching T.V. and visiting. Then her family excused themselves and went to bed.

When we got sleepy, we went into Carol's room. We stayed up, playing show tunes on the record player. She was especially fond of *Once Upon a Mattress* and *Carousel*. We were softly singing along, careful not to wake anyone. Then we put on our jammies and got into our beds—she in hers and me in her sister's.

We were talking back and forth between the beds, reliving the high points of the evening and having a good time. All of a sudden, I was

26

overcome with a powerful need to be close to her. I got out of her sister's bed, walked over and got into bed with her. It felt like the most natural thing in the world. At the same time, I knew it was an outrageous thing for me to be doing.

Carol and I often hugged but this was our first time lying in bed together. It felt so good to be lying next to her. It stirred something new within me—a feeling of excitement. The natural smell of her skin made me feel comfy and warm. From that day forward, it would bring me to a state of sexual arousal.

I leaned over and kissed her, a little bit nervous that she might pull away. I was relieved when she didn't resist. I had never lay in bed with *anyone*—guy or girl. It felt so good to be that close to Carol while wearing only our pajamas. It was so intimate.

As we lay there in each other's arms, kissing and hugging, it seemed to me that my feelings were reciprocated by Carol. I felt that same special something we had between us as friends—only a more intense version. Having this new dimension added to our already close friendship was so special. It was heaven for me.

I felt really happy but also very nervous. I knew that Carol's parents could walk in at any moment and catch us like that. They had a habit of knocking and then entering without waiting for an invitation.

As we lay in bed together, I was acutely aware of the fact that what we were doing together wasn't considered normal—not by my parents and not by anyone else, for that matter. I was supposed to be with a boy, not a girl.

What am I going to do now? I asked myself. *What happens from here?*

Only later would I find out that Carol was so scared, she wanted to stop—but we were enjoying the moment too much.

Our hugging and kissing started with our jammies on and progressed to a sexual place, with us touching each other underneath our jammies. (They never came off; we were too scared that her parents might walk in on us.) Even as our relationship turned sexual, it remained delicate and innocent. (I would later realize that all those times that Carol had lain with her head on my lap were actually the first signs of sexual tension between us.)

After the interlude, I went back over to her sister's bed and slept there. I knew in that moment that my life would never be the same. I felt so wonderful inside, and so good about myself for mustering up the courage to join Carol in her bed. I had surprised myself by being the aggressor. Then again, I knew that Carol would never have initiated anything between us. She was too shy.

Once we were back in separate beds, we were both very quiet. We processed our feelings privately and fell asleep. Even as I was filled with these exciting new feelings, I was frightened over what might happen next.

The following morning, a Saturday, we were very shy with each other. The intimacy of the night before had changed our friendship into something else. What that might be was still up in the air. We couldn't even look each other in the eye. Suddenly the ease and comfort we had always felt with each other was replaced with awkwardness and uncertainty.

We weren't unsure of our *feelings* for each other. We simply had no idea how our new relationship was going to fit into our lives—or into society. It was the very first time either of us had been intimate with another person, male or female. (I'd had that one moment with Molly when I was nine years old. But, I was so young at the time, I didn't even consider it to be part of my life experience.)

The entire world had changed for us overnight. Even the environment took on a different atmosphere. It was hard to know what to do with ourselves. Everything was so new. We made our way out into the living room to join Carol's family. Since it was a weekend morning, the family would be having breakfast together.

Now Carol and I had to figure out how to appear normal in front of her parents. We suddenly went from not being able to look at each other to not being able to look at her parents. Carol's sister Arline was also at the breakfast table.

Carol and I had a big secret and we instinctively understood that it had to remain exactly that. We couldn't tell a soul—not even our friends. The secret we shared bound us together and enabled us to overcome our awkwardness. We had more immediate concerns than our shyness with each other. Our top priority in that moment, and in the days to come, was to keep our families (and everyone else) from figuring out the truth about us.

At that point, we didn't yet have a clear idea of what that truth *was* or whether there was a name for it. We did know enough to know that it wouldn't be well received. The expectation from our parents was that we would avoid sleeping with *anyone* until we were married. Of course, the assumption was that we would be tempted by boys—not each other.

Five

Even before my intimate interlude with Carol, I already loved her dearly as a friend. Now there was this added dimension that enhanced our bond. My feelings for her were stronger than ever and I knew that I wanted to be with her. I also knew that this was what was right for me—that Carol was the one for me.

At the same time, the idea of being with a woman—or any two women being together, for that matter!—was completely foreign to me. I had never known or even *seen* a couple comprised of two women.

When I got home after that life-changing night and walked in the door of our apartment, I knew what I had to do. I had to keep my relationship with Carol a secret from my family. I had never kept secrets from my parents, but I felt I had no choice. I knew with absolute certainty that they would never understand or approve. I was sleeping with someone and having relations without being married. To make matters worse, that someone was a girl, not a boy.

Feeling that I had to keep this secret about Carol left me in a strange position. I knew that if I dwelled on the fact that I couldn't be honest with my parents and my siblings, I would never be able to stop thinking about it. I had always been that way. Once I started thinking about something, I would turn it over and over in my mind and become obsessed with it.

So, I began to develop inside myself the ability to compartmentalize. I would tuck something away inside myself so completely, it left my consciousness.

I saw my parents standing in the kitchen but I couldn't face them. I walked right past them and into my bedroom. This was unusual behavior for me.

Mom followed me into my room. "Are you okay, Arlene?"

"Yes, I'm okay," I said, not offering any further explanation.

I knew I had done something that would be considered wrong by my parents. But according to *me,* it was not only right but beautiful and wonderful. That doesn't mean for one second that I understood what was happening between me and Carol. I was sure of my feelings but baffled as to what it all meant.

When Carol and I were just friends, we were completely carefree. We got along wonderfully and everything was smooth. Now that our relationship had moved into romantic territory, there were so many new things to consider and so many new feelings we had to manage.

After Mom left my room, I stayed in there for a while. I needed to think about what had happened and process my feelings. I had recently broken up with Otto, a boy. I didn't understand why I was now interested in a girl—but I was and there was no getting around it. I went back and forth in my mind.

I was brought up to be with a boy, I said to myself. *And now with I'm with a girl. What's going to happen?*

In the years that I was going with Otto, I always felt good when I was kissing him. Having someone hold me and kiss me was satisfying in and of itself. I never had any physical desire or urge to "go all the way." I never even thought about it.

Even if I *had* thought about it, I would have been careful to avoid doing anything more than kissing. I didn't want to do anything that might give me a bad reputation again.

It wasn't just Otto, either, who failed to inspire sexual feelings in me. I never had the same feelings with any boy that I did with Carol. I loved how soft she was and how fresh she smelled.

I was feeling scared, but I couldn't turn to my parents for reassurance or comfort. I was accustomed to telling them everything, but there was no way I could bring this up. Since I was afraid of letting something slip out in conversation, I became very careful about what I discussed with them. As a result, the dynamic between us changed completely.

As time went by, I went from being totally open and honest with my parents to lying on a regular basis. I lied to them about where I was going and who was going to be with me. As Carol and I got closer and closer, I disconnected from them more and more. They could sense that my relationship with them had shifted but they must have been afraid to ask me about it directly.

I'm not sure they wanted to hear the reason. I do know that they would never in a million years have attributed the distance between us to the fact that I was in a romantic relationship with my best friend. Such a thing was not within their realm of thought. I was very feminine and Mom knew I had dated Otto for four years. There was no reason why she would think I was seeing a girl.

Even though I was disconnected and alienated from my parents as it concerned who I was spending time with, we maintained a good relationship otherwise. I compartmentalized the lying and hiding I was doing related to Carol. I also continued to maintain good relationships with both my sister and brother but revealed nothing to them about my relationship with Carol, either.

No one in the family acknowledged any of the awkwardness. I knew I wasn't the only one feeling it. Yet, everyone went about their business as if nothing had changed. I had no idea what my parents or siblings might have been thinking or feeling.

It was one thing to experience awkward silences at Carol's house. They were used to eating meals together without speaking or talking to each other about their day. But, it was strange and uncomfortable to have that kind of quietness in my house. We were loud and conversational with each other.

From then on, it was Carol and me all the time. We were a twosome and we isolated ourselves as much as we could. When we were with other friends, we tried to behave like our connection was nothing more than a friendship. I had no idea how well our charade was working. I do know that we spent a lot of time around Gloria and Janet, and they never appeared to notice any romantic feelings between Carol and me. Or, if they did, they kept it to themselves.

Carol was still working at Korvettes, but I had left by then. I never intended to stay on permanently. It was only an interim job for me. I was now working for a company called Women's American ORT ("Rehab Through Training"). In my role at ORT, I was the assistant to the bookkeeper.

In accepting this job, my thinking was, *Since I didn't go to college, at least I'll have the training I get from this job. That will be good for me. And maybe I can move up and be promoted to a higher position.*

Carol had always been insecure, uncomfortable in her skin, and self-conscious about her curly hair. She worried about the fact that she looked less feminine than I did. She felt more vulnerable to being exposed.

Of course, if you had asked either one of us in those early days what we were afraid of being exposed *as*, we would have shrugged. We were, as I said, completely unaware of any relationship that wasn't comprised of a man and a woman.

Work was the one area where Carol was most worried about being found out. She was petrified that someone would discover her secret. Over time, she would go to incredible lengths to keep the secret hidden. Neither one of us had any idea just how much of a toll it would take on her.

Around this time, my family and Carol's moved, along with the rest of the Jewish tribe that had moved to Castle Hill together. Co-op City, our new development, was in the Bronx on the way upstate. It was a subsidized development but, being a co-op, all the families owned a little piece of the property. Co-op City was comprised of thirty buildings of varying sizes. The complex was less uniform than Castle Hill and yet I still managed to get lost there.

We finally had air-conditioning, which was glorious. So, our rooms were nice and cool when we slept over at each other's apartments. We had kept up our sleepovers even after our friendship turned romantic. We figured our best bet was to continue doing what we had always done. We didn't want to draw any attention to ourselves by making an abrupt change.

In the evenings after dinner, Carol and I had always hung out with the group of young people at the complex where we lived. Once we got to Co-op City, that all stopped. I was absolutely obsessed with her and we spent all our time together. As far as what we told our parents, however, we were still hanging out with the crowd.

Those times we pretended to be hanging out with the crowd usually involved us going off together. It would be just the two of us in the car. Sometimes we drove around town. If we went out to eat, we would usually take a back booth where we were less likely to be seen.

Once in a while, we drove all the way to Connecticut and checked into a hotel. In those days, you could still pay for hotel rooms with cash. We paid for the rooms from our own salaries, and our parents were never the wiser. They didn't keep tabs on how much money we were bringing home or how we spent our paychecks.

Carol would tell her parents that she was sleeping at my house and I would tell mine that I was sleeping at hers. All it would have taken was one phone call between our parents for the whole thing to blow up in our faces. We were playing with fire.

We always passed ourselves off as cousins. As we walked up to the desk to check into a hotel, we would be careful to look straight ahead. We knew better than to risk a glance at each other. Our feelings would have been written all over our faces.

I was much more comfortable in my skin than Carol, and much more at ease with our relationship. I was sure of our relationship and knew we'd be together forever. I still had many questions related to how our relationship with each other would play out in the real world, but it never caused me the level of anxiety it caused Carol.

The worst-case scenario in Carol's mind was that somebody would find out, expose us to everyone we knew, and then everyone would shun us. When it came to her family, friends, coworkers and colleagues, she was especially terrified of exposure. I understood her fears and shared them to a minor extent. But I was able to live with those fears without them causing me much discomfort.

As I said, neither Carol nor I had ever so much as heard of a same-sex relationship at that time. We would later find out that they did exist but were kept very hush-hush and behind closed doors. There may not have been an actual law against them but there was certainly a societal prohibition. There certainly was no pride about it, like there is today with nationwide pride parades and events. And there *was* a law against same-sex marriage.

The very fact that such a thing was rare, or at least uncommon and hidden, made our imaginations run wild. We had no idea what might actually happen if we were found out. It was the fear of the unknown that was so hard to live with, especially for Carol. Monsters under the bed are always more terrifying than those staring us right in the eye.

Six

I could tell how hard it was on Carol to be with me. She felt she was supposed to be with a boy and was always terribly conflicted over it. It made me sad to know how much anxiety she carried related to our relationship. Our love was supposed to be a beautiful thing, and it was, but for Carol there was always fear and anxiety that went along with it.

I always felt badly that I didn't experience the same deep fears and concerns that Carol did. I didn't worry that someone would find out about us and shun us. I was a little afraid but mostly because *she* was afraid. I was comfortable with myself. I figured that, if our friends did find out about us, I would be able to sit them down and explain the situation.

As for my family, they were generally very understanding and pretty open—not that they were ever involved with anyone who was gay or LGBTQ+. But I felt that they would have understood that I was in love with someone, regardless of whether it was a man or woman.

It always seemed like there was a higher risk for Carol than for me. Our parents were the same age, but hers were much more old school than mine—and very strict. Not only was she afraid to tell them anything, she was also shy about revealing her feelings to them. They were not the type of people who would ever sit down and talk things out.

Carol had a strange closeness with her parents but much of their bond was unspoken. Any time Carol saw her mother upset, she cried. She was deeply empathetic towards her mother—and afraid of her at the same time. Carol's father was very old-world European, which made sense considering that he was in his mother's belly when she emigrated to America. He was brought up by European parents and carried that sensibility even though he was born in the States.

One day when Carol and I were sitting in her red Corvair, I said, "I think it's time for us to move out so we can be together and have private time."

She looked at me like I had suggested we jump off the roof together. "I can't do that!"

"We have to! It's time to move out. I'm going to tell my parents I'm moving out," I said. "There's nothing wrong with two friends moving in together."

"How can we move out?" she said. "We're not married! We're not allowed to move out until we're married."

She was right. Single Jewish girls did not move out of their parents' homes until they were married. In those days, *no* young women—Jewish or otherwise—rented apartments together as roommates.

That didn't stop me. I was always a trendsetter. I knew what I felt was right and that was all there was to it. "We're just two friends moving out!" I insisted. "We're twenty-two years old, not married, not seeing anybody but each other and we need to move out!" I said.

In order to sneak away to see Carol, I had been telling my parents that I was going out and meeting up with a young man.

My parents would say, "Well, bring him by the house so we can meet him."

"No, no…I have to meet him somewhere." I would say.

A year or so before this conversation about moving out, Carol told me, "My parents set me up on a blind date. I feel like I have to go to keep up appearances."

"Are you kidding me? You're going out with someone else?" I was jealous and hurt. I was also worried that she might go out with this guy and decide that she wanted to be with a guy instead of with me. It made me feel very insecure and I didn't like the feeling at all.

"My parents are always questioning me!" she said. "Yours leave you alone. If I don't go, they won't understand. I'll never hear the end of it."

Her parents had been saying to her, "You're twenty-two and you should be married! Everyone is married by twenty-two. What's going on?"

While Carol was at the ballgame with the nice Jewish guy her mom had set her up with, I cried. I didn't stop until she got home.

When they got home from their date, Carol came to see me. "I didn't feel anything for him at all. I just had to go because of my mother."

On the one hand, I felt reassured. On the other hand, I remained a little bit insecure. I never would have gone on a date with anyone else, even if my parents insisted. I was bothered by the fact that Carol agreed to go. It made me feel like she could one day decide she might have to be with a boy in order to make her parents happy. I didn't express my insecurities to her but they stayed with me.

After listening to me try to talk her into moving out with me, Carol finally gave in. "Okay," she said, "I'm going upstairs to tell my parents I'm moving out. You stay here and wait. I'll come back and tell you how it went."

The minutes crawled by as I waited in the car for her to come back downstairs. After what was probably half an hour but felt like all day, I saw her come downstairs.

"I didn't tell them," she said, sitting beside me in the car. "I couldn't. I knew they wouldn't understand. They don't want me to move out until I'm married."

"But, why didn't you at least try?"

"I can't do that to my parents...especially not to my mother."

Carol was very close to her mother, and knew it would have broken her heart.

Now it was my heart that was broken. "We *have* to move out!" I said.

"No," she said, "we're not moving out."

"I can't do this anymore," I said. "Somebody will find out if we don't move out. I'm afraid one of our moms will walk in on us or something. Or someone will notice something. We can only tempt fate for so long!" I was crying my eyes out.

Carol remained steadfast in her position. She absolutely refused.

"Do you really love me?" I asked. "If you stay here with your parents rather than moving out with me, how can I feel like you really love me?"

"I do love you! But I can't do it now. Maybe when we're twenty-five."

"Twenty-five! That's three years from now! That's a long time."

"It's the way it has to be," she insisted.

For a couple of hours, she was ready to give up on us. I was crying and trying to hold our relationship together.

There was no precedent for me proposing that we move in together. So, it naturally made Carol nervous and anxious when she thought about bringing it up to her parents. We were supposed to marry men and have children.

Even if I had married a man instead of falling in love with Carol, I might never have had children. Mom always had me take care of the foster babies in the house. That gave me plenty of time to discover whether or not I had the urge to have children. The truth was, I didn't seem to care one way or another whether or not I ever had children of my own. Maybe my instinctive maternal needs were satisfied by looking after the foster babies and helping with my own sister and Heidi.

Carol talked about having children. Given that the concept of two women being together as a couple was still taboo, there was no avenue for two women having children together.

"Well, if we're not moving out," I said, "then we have to go on a trip so we can have some alone time. We never get to be alone for any length of time like we would if we lived together."

She thought about it for a minute and then she said, "Okay…let's talk about taking a trip."

We were both working, so we had the money to travel. And, neither one of us ran into any problems when we told our parents that we were going on vacation together. My parents liked Carol and hers liked me very much. Of course, they thought of us as nothing more than two close friends.

We took a fifteen-day trip to Europe. As usual, we posed as cousins. Including first-class airfare, our trip only cost us a thousand dollars each. We went to Lisbon where armed guards with rifles stood sentry on every corner of the city. We had no idea why they were posted there. We figured there must have been some sort of conflict going on in nearby Spain.

Carol and I stayed in a tiny hotel in a room on a high floor. We had a view of the entire city. For breakfast, we had hot rolls with butter—a continental breakfast. We saw the Blue Grotto by boat. We had to lie down as the boat passed beneath the rocks on its way into the Blue Grotto. We were rewarded with the most beautiful sight—the clearest, bluest water we had ever seen in our lives.

We also spent some time in Madrid. It seemed like a big city, like New York. But at three o'clock each afternoon, the town shut down so that everyone could take a siesta.

In Italy we saw the Pieta sculpture and went to the Vatican. When we got to the Sistine Chapel and looked up at the ceiling, I wondered, *How in the world did Michelangelo paint such a magnificent work of art while lying on his back on a ladder?*

While we were on vacation, I was in a good mood because I now knew that we were not breaking up. And I also knew in my heart that we would move in together eventually. I was reassured when Carol said that she might be willing to move out when we were twenty-five. Meanwhile, Carol was happy and relaxed on our trip because I had stopped pressuring her to move out.

Carol was a big history buff. Her favorite part of the trip was touring the ruins in Italy. I had a take-it-or-leave-it attitude toward the ruins, but I was happy to see her having such a good time. The things I would remember most vividly about our European vacation were the Blue Grotto and the view of the water from our hotel room.

My very favorite thing about our trip was the fact that Carol and I got to have all that alone time together, without worrying that we might be questioned or found out. As far as anyone in Europe knew, we were simply two female cousins on vacation together.

Seven

Our fifteen-day trip felt like it lasted a lifetime. Having had the luxury of so much alone time with Carol, I was in a great state of mind as we headed back home. I didn't want it to end. I knew that when we got home, we would have to resume our routine of spending only stolen moments together.

Our flight was smooth and uneventful. When we landed at the airport, my dad picked us up. He was warm and at ease around Carol and me, as always. I can't say it enough—my father truly was the most wonderful person in the world. I think when you grow up in an orphanage, as he did, you either become embittered or you set out to find what you didn't have and give it to your own family. I am so lucky my dad fell into the second category.

I noticed that Dad had a knowing look in his eye. *He knows about Carol and me. He must feel it.*

Even though I had a feeling that my dad already knew, I didn't dare confirm his suspicions. He and my mother had no secrets between them. So, he would have felt compelled to tell her. It was a struggle, knowing that I was constantly lying to my parents.

When we got home, we dropped off Carol. Then I prepared myself to go inside our apartment.

"Did you have a good time?" Mom asked.

I was careful not to make eye contact with my mom. I couldn't risk revealing what was happening between Carol and me and how I was feeling about her. I was being careful more for Carol than myself, knowing how paranoid she was about anyone finding out about us.

"Yes, we had a wonderful time," I said, trying to keep my tone light and carefree.

"Did you meet any nice boys?"

"No…" I decided not to make up a European boyfriend. "There were no interesting boys on the tour." (Carol and I had been traveling with a tour group and all of our activities were very structured.)

In actuality, I had guys hitting on me all the time, especially in Europe. They would see Carol and me and assume exactly what we wanted them to assume—that we were two friends or cousins, traveling together.

One day in Italy, a cute olive-skinned guy with dark curly hair approached Carol and me and the three of us starting talking. In broken English, he asked me if I would like to go out with him that evening.

"No," I said, "I can't. I'm busy."

It made me feel good to know that I was attractive to guys—but at the same time, it made me feel badly for Carol. Guys never hit on her. I didn't want her getting her feelings hurt when she saw them hitting on me. More importantly, I didn't want her to worry that her secret wasn't as well hidden as she thought. She radiated more of her true sexual orientation than I did. Guys picked up on it, if only subconsciously.

We were twenty-two years old and still rarely going out in public together. We were not like our other friends in their early twenties who spent a lot of time in nightclubs. From time to time, we agreed to accompany our friends to straight nightclubs, but we weren't relaxed or at home in those places.

Mostly we stayed at Carol's house or mine, spent time with friends, or went away on trips. I always told my parents the truth whenever Carol and I were going out of town together. Thankfully, that was one thing I didn't need to lie about. It was completely believable to my parents that my best friend and I were taking a trip together.

Our favorite nearby getaway was Atlantic City. We would check into a motel where we liked to stay. Then I went and got powdered donuts and coffee from the lobby and brought them to Carol on a tray. Sometimes we spent all day snuggled up in bed with our coffee and donuts, watching cartoons together.

It was glorious knowing that it was just the two of us in a room by ourselves, with the door locked. When we were ready to venture outside, we walked along the boardwalk, rode bikes, and explored the little shops.

Then Carol and I found out about a lesbian nightclub. "Oh, my God!" I said. "Look at this! There's a nightclub just for women."

"What? Where is it?" said Carol.

"In a loft in the city. Downtown. Should we go?"

"Well…if you want to go, I'm okay with it," said Carol.

"Really? Are you sure?"

"Yes, we can go if you want to."

"I'm so surprised and happy you want to go!"

We agreed that we would leave right away if it turned out to be too much for us. Thankfully, now that we were in our twenties, it was enough for us to tell our parents that we were going out. We didn't have to account for our whereabouts. Of course, if one of our parents asked us directly, we would make up something believable. Sometimes it even contained a kernel of truth.

We found the building in Manhattan. As we got into the elevator and pressed the button, I turned to Carol and said, "I'm really scared!"

"I'm more scared than you are!"

"I know!" I said. "And I'm so proud of you for agreeing to come."

I knew how afraid Carol was of being outed. The truth was, this women's club was one of the few public places where we *weren't* in any danger of being outed. Everyone there was in the same boat.

As the elevator doors opened and we entered the club, we knew we were taking a huge step. We were immediately surrounded by a sea of beautiful female couples. Carol and I looked at each other in total shock. We couldn't believe what we were seeing.

Up until that very moment, we had lived our lives like we were the only two women in the entire world who were in love with each other. We had never seen anyone else like us. We suspected that they were out there somewhere. Now, here was a nightclub filled with living proof.

We noticed a little alcove out of the way and wandered toward it in a daze. Once we took a seat, we remained glued to our chairs for the rest of the evening.

"Can you even believe this club exists?" we said to each other.

We were both overwhelmed. We had to really go out of our way to find that women's club. Before seeing it with our own eyes, we had been sheltered and naïve, living in our own little world.

Both Carol and I were incredibly happy over this discovery. It felt really good to know that we weren't the only two women in a same-sex relationship. Of course, it wasn't called a same-sex relationship back then. It wasn't called anything. Its existence wasn't acknowledged at all.

Neither Carol nor I mingled that night or spoke one word to any of the other women. We didn't dance. We didn't go up to the bar for drinks. We sat there like little kids, watching everybody around us with utter fascination. This was the first chance Carol and I had ever had to see our reflection in the mirror of these lesbian couples.

I felt almost voyeuristic, as we sat there observing. Carol was having the exact same experience, only more so, due to her insecurities. It was an out-of-body experience.

Is this the way it's supposed to be? I asked myself. *Women being together in couples like this? Is this supposed to happen like this?*

From time to time, we would lean in and whisper to each other a few words about the scene unfolding around us. After an hour and a half or so, we got up and left. As we walked out onto the street, we were overwhelmed with many emotions. It was hard to articulate what we were feeling, much less understand it.

"Some of those women were openly hugging and kissing!" I remarked. "They were really demonstrative."

"I know…" said Carol. "It was kind of uncomfortable watching it, wasn't it?"

"Yeah, for me too…"

Of course, Carol and I had a sexual relationship ourselves. For some reason, that didn't keep it from being any less strange to see other women openly expressing affection. We had simply never seen it before. Both in real life and in the movies, women kissed men—not each other. So, the visual of women kissing and hugging each other was quite foreign to us.

We were almost staggering as we walked to the subway station. We both felt the enormous impact of discovering that there were many other couples like us. It was reassuring on the one hand and jarring on the other. It forced us to take a hard look at ourselves and question what we were doing.

I was conflicted over what I was seeing. It just didn't look normal to me. I found it disconcerting, despite the fact that Carol and I shared an intimate relationship in private.

"How could this be right here in New York City?" we asked each other.

When we got back home, I slept over at her place. We lay in the dark, talking about what we had experienced that night—she in her bed, and me in her sister's. We tried to sort it all out.

"Does this make things different for you, knowing there are other people like us?" I asked.

"Yes," she said. "It makes a difference between the two of us because now we can feel like there are other people like us. So, we're normal. But it doesn't make a difference as far as me telling people about us."

Before we fell asleep, we talked about the possibility of moving in together in a few years.

"For now," I said, "I guess we just have to bide our time."

"Yes," she agreed, "I can't move out until I'm twenty-five."

I made my way into her bed and we held each other. The evening had been too momentous for us to sleep apart. I needed to feel close to her. Her parents never walked in on us at night; there would have been no reason to enter Carol's room. Her sister was sleeping on the couch, and the household was dark.

There was, however, always the chance that Carol's parents might walk in on us in the morning. We couldn't let ourselves be discovered sleeping in the same bed. I always made sure to make my way back into her sister's bed before sleep overtook me. As long as I was careful not to fall asleep in her bed, we were safe.

When we slept at my house, it was different. My mother did not like closed doors and thought nothing of walking into my bedroom unannounced.

It would be an interesting few years as we counted down the months until we turned twenty-five and could move out of our parents' homes. Trying not to get caught together kept us in a constant state of low-level anxiety.

Carol and I continued to take our trips to Atlantic City for alone time. We visited Provincetown on Cape Cod, and New Hampshire, as well. We also attended many weddings together, including the wedding of our friend Gloria. (Carol, Janet, Gloria and I were still a close foursome of friends.)

I didn't really enjoy attending weddings. From time to time, we were invited to them and couldn't say no. We were almost always the only two single girls. No one thought anything of Carol and me attending together—just two female friends (or cousins) without dates.

Attending with each other instead of with guys meant that we had no one to dance with at the reception. We were able to do the fast dances together without raising any eyebrows, but we had to sit out the slow dances. If a guy asked one of us to dance, we usually accepted, just to blend in. It was always hard on me to see Carol dancing with a guy.

Our friend Andy also got married, and Carol and I were both asked to be bridesmaids. It was an absolutely beautiful Greek Orthodox wedding—but both the ceremony and the reception went on forever. Carol and I both felt awkward and really wanted to leave. As bridesmaids, we had to stay until it was over. We kept fending off guys who wanted to slow dance with us. We had to occasionally say yes, just to keep up appearances.

These weddings always drove home the reality that I would never get to have the wedding of my dreams. I didn't care one way or another about having children—but it made me sad when I thought about never having a wedding with Carol.

I would sit there and think, *I really want a wedding and it's too bad we'll never be able to have one. No one will ever celebrate our love. We'll always have to keep it a secret.*

Eight

At last, Carol and I turned twenty-five. The time had come to move out.

"You should tell your parents first," I told Carol.

We both knew that her parents would take the news much harder than mine. We wanted to get that out of the way first.

Carol got up her nerve and went to break the news to them.

I was at home, watching the clock, waiting on Carol to come over and tell me how the news had gone over. (My own parents were away at the moment; they may have been at my grandparents' house.)

I heard the knock at the door and opened it.

Carol was standing there, sobbing. "It was awful. My mom couldn't stop crying. She told me it was not okay for me to move out. But I'm doing it anyway."

Her parents cried bitterly and she cried right along with them. She was deeply empathetic when it came to her parents. When they hurt, she hurt. This was especially true between her and her mother because they were so close. When Carol's mother was having a problem, she was having a problem.

(Understandably, Carol's mother would end up being very distraught on moving day. I intentionally stayed out of the way that day. I didn't want my presence to make things any harder on Carol. I knew that her parents liked me. I also knew that they didn't want their daughter

49

leaving home until she was married. I felt that my presence might have made things worse.)

"What did they say to you?" I asked.

"My mom said, 'No! We don't want you to go! We don't understand why you have to leave. You're not leaving to get married! Just stay home with us until you meet somebody and get married.'"

"What did you tell them?" I asked.

"I said, 'I am twenty-five, and working full time. Arlene and I want to get a place together.'" Carol was choking back tears.

"What did your father say?" I asked.

"He didn't say anything. He was just really grumpy."

"I'm so proud of you for doing it! And, I'm so sorry about how they reacted, but you shouldn't be surprised."

I was upset for Carol. Her parents never did give her the green light to move out. It's hard to say what gave her the courage to make the move anyway, given how resistant she had been only a handful of years earlier. Maybe she simply needed those years to get used to the idea that she was going to be moving out against her parents' wishes.

Before my parents came home, Carol left. Now it was my turn. Back when Carol and I were twenty-two and I was trying to talk her into moving out with me, I told my parents that I planned to leave. They were fine with it then, and they were fine with it now that Carol and I were twenty-five. In fact, they were glad that I was planning to share an apartment with someone they knew so well. They accepted the announcement calmly and there was no big emotional scene.

Afterwards, Carol asked me, "So, what happened with your parents?"

"Everything went fine," I said. "They were sad but they didn't make a scene. But Heidi did…She kept begging me to stay with her. I tried to explain to her, 'Heidi, I'm twenty-five years old now, and it's time for me to move out and start my own life. I can't live here forever.'"

Heidi was only ten years old when I moved out. She was still just a little girl. I had practically raised her, and we were very close. I understood why she would be upset over me moving out.

Now that we had told our families about our plans, it was time to figure out where we wanted to live. We had already looked at a few different apartment buildings in the Bronx and knew that we didn't want to stay there. We were ready for a new neighborhood.

We both worked in Manhattan at Korvettes but we couldn't afford to live right in the city. (Carol had stayed at Korvettes and been promoted to different stores over time. I had left at one point but was working there for the second time.) We decided to look at places in Flushing, Queens. That way, we would have an easy commute over the bridge.

We found a cute, affordable apartment in a brand-new, four-story, twenty-four-unit building. We introduced ourselves to the building manager as cousins. If the manager found it strange for two twenty-five-year-old women to be renting an apartment together in an era when it just wasn't done, she kept it to herself.

In looking back, it amazes me that we were able to pass as cousins all those years. We didn't look remotely alike. Carol's hair was very curly and mine was straight. She had olive skin and mine was light. She was thin with green eyes and I was heavier with hazel eyes.

There was only one catch—the apartment we wanted wouldn't be ready for a month. We felt that it was worth waiting for. We knew we could both stay living at home while it was readied for us. So, we put down a deposit on the place and waited.

Unlike the huge buildings we had both always lived in with our parents, this one had a lot of character. Best of all, it was located in a block at the top of a hill, so we knew we would have a good view. And we liked the fact that it was situated near stores, a bakery, and the bridge into the city.

We liked the outside of the building and fell in love with the unit itself. We were predisposed to loving the place simply because it was going to afford us the privacy we had been wanting for so long. It also happened to be a genuinely cute apartment.

From the front door looking straight ahead into the living room, you could see the windows. For the living room we bought a beige sectional couch. The kitchen was on the left and was very narrow. I liked the appliances and the fact that everything was shiny and white. On the right was a little dining area which we furnished with a bistro-style dinette set.

To the right of the living room was a spacious bedroom and bathroom. Given that we had to keep up the charade of being cousins and best friends, there was no way we were going to be able to put a queen bed in the bedroom. So, we brought the twin beds we had slept in while growing up and put those in there. Carol and I were so happy to have our own apartment, we wouldn't have cared if we'd had to sleep on the floor.

We couldn't believe we finally had our own place with our own furniture. We really put our hearts into fixing it up. We had our new couch and bistro table and chairs, and now it was time to do something about the white walls. They looked too institutional and reminded us of the buildings where we both grew up.

We painted our bedroom walls a soothing medium blue, and wallpapered the little dining area. Then we hung spider plants by the windows. (We didn't have drapes but we did have blinds on the windows.)

All in all, the place looked very homey. Having a cozy little place with Carol was perfect. As far as I was concerned, the smaller the better. It had been five long years of hiding and pretending and it had finally come to an end. We were both thrilled to have this new beginning. At last we had the sanctuary we had been longing for since we first got together.

At night, we tied the legs of our twin beds together and turned it into one big bed. To eliminate the feeling of the separation between the twin beds, we used a mattress pad made just for that purpose. It had a piece that fit between the two beds.

We knew that, if we wanted to protect our little nest, we were going to have to continue to keep up appearances. So, we developed a habit of removing the mattress pad and pushing the beds apart each morning. I don't think we slept a wink that first night. We were too excited.

A week or so after we moved in, I walked into the bathroom and discovered a big water bug on the floor. I screamed and grabbed a can of hairspray. After dousing the bug with hair spray, I ran out of the bedroom with a towel which I placed under the crack of the door.

When Christmastime of 1972 rolled around, Carol insisted we get a Christmas tree. I said, "A Christmas tree? But we're Jewish!"

Working in retail at Korvettes, Carol was surrounded by Christmas decorations all day long. She found it all enchanting.

I wasn't a Christmas person. Having a tree went against all the beliefs my parents had raised me with, and all our traditions. At the same time, the experience of having to stand outside synagogue services because my family couldn't afford the membership fee had left me with little love for religion. So, I figured, *If Carol wants a Christmas tree, it's fine with me.*

Neither one of us had ever bought a Christmas tree before. We had no idea what we were doing. We went with a fake, four-foot-tall green tree, and bought red, green and silver ornaments and tinsel. We chose a tree that wasn't overly large. We had to be prepared to move the tree into the bathtub when we had company come over. We made sure the shower curtain was opaque enough to conceal the tree hidden in the tub.

We couldn't tell our parents (or hers, anyway) that we were getting a Christmas tree. And, we certainly didn't want them to walk in and see it in the living room. The odds seemed slim that they would use the bathroom while visiting us, and pull back the shower curtain in the tub.

When my parents came to visit our new apartment around the winter holidays, I didn't bother to hide the tree.

"Why do you have a tree?" they asked.

"It's not religious," I said. "Christmas is all over the store when we go to work. And we like the feeling of all the lights and decorations and wanted to bring some of it home with us."

My parents didn't have strong feelings about us having a tree and quickly dropped the subject.

We decided that since we had already decorated our apartment for Christmas, we needed to really celebrate. That meant opening presents on Christmas morning. We also celebrated Hanukkah at both her parents' apartment and mine. For the Hanukkah meal, we had roasted chicken and latkes with applesauce and sour cream.

In keeping with tradition, we had presents for each night of Hanukkah. They were nothing extravagant—just trinkets. My parents didn't have much money and I never had expectations. I treasured every little gift they gave me.

It was wonderful seeing my siblings at the Hanukkah get-together. We had lived together for so long and I had truly missed them once I moved out. My brother was in military service at the time. Phyllis never showed much emotion toward me or anyone else, but she was happy to see me.

Heidi and I were very happy to see each other, and she was distraught as I left. She sobbed and reminded me of the time I put a soft stuffed rabbit in her arms while she was sleeping. It must have been a comforting memory. She brought it up often.

Nine

Carol and I only stayed in our cozy little apartment for two years. The building never did get the water-bug problem under control. In 1974, it finally drove us out. We didn't go far—only a few blocks away, and closer to the interstate.

Our new place was in a twenty-seven-story building, with twelve units per floor. It was located near Flushing Meadow Park, and was originally built to accommodate travelers in town for the 1964 World's Fair. Best of all, the rent was on par with what we had been paying in the previous building.

When we walked into the available unit on the twenty-third floor, we were taken by the spectacular view from the windows. Because we were high up, we could keep the blinds open and still have complete privacy. The bedroom was huge and we loved it—not that we could put a queen bed in it. Our twin beds followed us wherever we went.

Living with Carol was the ultimate. I had my very best friend as my roommate, and we were also in love and sexually intimate. I had everything I needed under one roof. In this apartment, we would end up having our best male friends, Tommy and John, living right above us, one floor up.

Carol and John had met at Korvettes before John and Tommy met and got together. One evening after work, Carol came home and said, "John came out to me today."

"Really? How fabulous! And then you told him about you and me?"

"No," said Carol. "I couldn't. He works for me! What if he said something to somebody at work? It wouldn't be good."

It felt absolutely wrong not to level with him. I thought to myself, *He cared so much about Carol, he told her his secret, yet there she was, not saying anything to him?*

"Carol, you would make him feel more comfortable if you told him!" I said. "It would make things easier for him. He's uncomfortable in his own skin because he's gay and hasn't come out to anybody. Now, he's told you. If you also tell him about yourself, you'll show him that he's not the only one. It will be better for him."

Carol was unconvinced. She was less attuned to people than I. It was harder for her to gauge when it would be safe to let her guard down. She was also generally more conservative and careful than I, and much more afraid of being found out.

I often tried to help her see that her fears were unfounded when it came to certain people discovering our secret. Sadly, nothing I said seemed to put her fears to rest.

I was very attuned to my friends, so it was easy for me to sense when it was safe to tell them about myself. I knew that not telling them would leave me in an awkward position where I had to speak about everything in general terms.

I would have to say, for example, "I went to a movie with a friend." It struck a false note and made me feel like I was lying by omission. Any time I had the chance to be relaxed and authentic, I took it.

All those years when I was still living at home and felt I needed to lie to my parents had been hard on me. We were *still* lying to our parents—just not on a daily basis, because we lived on our own and had less occasion to see them. I didn't want to be lying to anybody in my life. I wanted to be honest about Carol and me.

I told Carol, "Look, if you won't tell John, then I'm going to tell him."

"No! You can't!"

"Carol, we can't *not* tell him. We're friends with him and he came out to you. There's no risk of anyone else finding out about us. Don't you see? He is expecting us to keep his secret and he would definitely keep ours."

I knew what was best for us. I *always* knew what was best for us, in terms of whether it was safe for us to say something to someone or whether the person would take it badly.

Sometimes Carol and I worked the same hours and sometimes we didn't. I waited until one wintry day when Carol was at work and I wasn't, and called John. I asked him if he would meet me so I could talk to him about something.

We met outside in the snow and said our hellos. "John, I have something to tell you. Carol told me that you came out to her…"

John looked at me in disbelief. Obviously, the last thing he expected was for Carol to tell me the secret he had shared with her. He stayed quiet, waiting to see where I was going with what I was saying.

"…Anyway, since you told Carol that *you* were gay, I wanted to tell you that Carol and I are in a relationship."

"I already knew," he said.

I was surprised by this.

"…When I came out to her," he said, "I was hoping she might say something to make it easier for me. When she didn't, I hoped that maybe you would say something. Because I already knew."

"I feel badly that she didn't say anything to you," I said. "It's because you work for her, and she's scared that you might tell someone. She's afraid of something bad happening if anyone at work finds out."

"I would never do that, Arlene."

"I know you wouldn't, John. Carol just gets scared. It has nothing to do with her not trusting you."

When Carol got home from work that day, I told her that I had told John. I thought she might be upset with me but she was glad I told him. She couldn't bring herself to tell him. The fear of something is often worse than the thing you're afraid of actually happening. So, once it was done and out in the open, Carol was fine with it.

I was relieved that she wasn't upset. "Now that he knows," I said, "you have the opportunity to be true friends with him. You won't have to feel uncomfortable anymore, worrying about him finding out about us. You can have a good, open relationship."

When the apartment right above us became available a couple of years later, Tommy and John moved in. Carol and I now had two confidantes, and that was a great relief to us. We became like the T.V. couples from *I Love Lucy* or *The Jackie Gleason Show*, living right near each other in the same apartment building. Only, those couples were straight and we were not.

I was already so happy living with Carol. Having Tommy and John living right upstairs was a great bonus. Being out to Tommy and John was one thing. Many more years would pass before we came out to our families, or anyone else for that matter. If it had been up to me, I would have been out to everyone.

I don't let much scare me. This fearlessness may have come from my upbringing. My parents were at ease within themselves and they fostered that same ease in me. They did not instill in me fear over anything. The fact that my family talked openly about things helped me feel fearless.

Even though my dad wasn't home a lot, he always made the time to talk to me. By talking things through, I learned to keep things in their proper proportion and perspective. I developed the belief that the danger is usually all in your head; it's not real.

Being raised to feel that the world was a safe place was what gave me the confidence to do whatever I felt like I should do at an early age. I didn't give anyone's opinion about what I should or shouldn't be doing any more credence than my own opinion. I had the final say on my life.

Carol, on the other hand, had an entirely different upbringing. She grew up in a house where nothing was brought out into the open. It's understandable how all those things that were being swept under the rug could take on monstrous proportions. No wonder she learned to be afraid.

When I was thirty-one years old, Carol, Tommy, John and I took a life-changing trip. Our vacation destination was in the Poconos—and it catered entirely to the LGBTQ+ population. When we heard about Rainbow Mountain, we couldn't believe that such a place actually existed anywhere but in our dreams. When we researched it and looked at pictures of it sitting atop a high mountain, we were instantly sold.

Carol and I agreed, "This looks so lovely! The four of us need to go."

Up until then, our one and only lesbian outing had been our trip to the women's club years earlier. It was thrilling to discover that there was a place where we could be surrounded by others like us. It was a place where we could be completely relaxed, without feeling the need to be undercover as cousins. We couldn't get there fast enough.

Rainbow Mountain was owned by two lesbians. They didn't have a huge budget to invest in the place, but they wanted to offer a safe place for those in the LGBTQ+ community. Lodging options included rooms in a vintage house, free-standing cabins, and motel-style rooms. We picked the motel rooms, which appeared to be newer, and made our reservations.

In those days, a vacation destination that was geared exclusively toward the LGBTQ+ community was nothing short of a miracle. For it to also have up-to-date and aesthetically pleasing accommodations was too much to hope for. We couldn't have cared less. We would have pitched a tent on Rainbow Mountain just to have a getaway where we could be ourselves. (Well, maybe not *a tent* for us city dwellers, but you get the point.)

Tommy and John booked a room next to ours at the motel and we all made the two-hour drive together. We had to drive up a narrow, winding road. During the entire drive, I kept thinking, *We're going to go flying right over the cliff at any minute!*

When we finally reached the top of the mountain, we saw a fabulous old house with a porch in front and little cabins all in a row. It looked just like the brochure. The four of us were both excited and nervous, given that it was our first time in a gay-only vacation destination. Having Tommy and John with us was comforting and I was glad they were there.

As we entered the house and approached the registration desk to sign in, overhead speakers were playing the theme from *Somewhere in Time*. We loved the song and the movie. It set a very romantic tone for our vacation.

I was glad that we had opted to stay in the motel rooms rather than the house. It had that musty smell you often find in old houses. We got our keys and made our way to our rooms. The rooms were nothing fancy. They were well beneath the aesthetic level we would normally find acceptable, especially for the price we were paying. But, since this was such a special outing, we were fine with our rooms.

We stayed for four or five days, not even wasting time unpacking our luggage. We were so excited to be there, we just lived out of our suitcases. There were several acres of verdant, beautiful property, and amazing views from the mountaintop. We took nature walks and played with the friendly sheepdog that ran free. (I've always loved dogs.)

There was a volleyball net in a concrete pool with a rainbow bottom. There were other guests in the pool, swimming and having fun. It was amazing for us to realize that every single person we saw on the property was gay. Seeing all these gay people in one place, enjoying themselves, was hard to process. We had gotten so used to living our lives in secret. The fact that Rainbow Mountain not only served the gay population but was also co-ed made it even more remarkable.

We sat on the patio of the gourmet restaurant at a table overlooking the pool, and had an incredible lunch together. It was such a big moment for us, and it had a dreamlike quality to it. We couldn't believe our eyes, as we saw other guests walking around, holding hands and kissing.

We kept saying to each other, "Can you believe we're here? With all these people just like us?"

It was the first time since Carol and I had gotten together that we felt included. Up until then, we were always a minority of two. It felt so good to be part of the community, and to have other people accept us. If we wanted to walk around holding hands or kissing, we could do so without getting strange looks from anyone or having to answer any unwanted questions.

Other than time spent together in our own apartment or with Tommy and John, we had never experienced that kind of freedom before. The feeling of freedom was echoed in the beauty of the environment—the sky felt bluer, the trees greener. Seeing Carol so relaxed and comfortable made it even more special.

We spent a lot of time in the pool. Sometimes we swam or lounged in the water. Sometimes the net was up so guests could play water volleyball. When the sun went down, we went to the barn to dance. Getting to dance with each other without being self-conscious was a real luxury.

We met new friends there. With every single person we met, the topic of conversation was the same: how freeing it was to be there. It was amazing getting to meet other same-sex couples. Our social lives had centered around the two of us and Tommy and John.

Up until then, it hadn't felt safe to meet new people. Now they were everywhere. Socializing with them was not only a possibility but a reality. We didn't have to go out of our way to find them. They were on the boats in the lake, and dancing beside us on the dance floor in the barn in the evenings. We smiled and said hello to each other in the restaurant.

On one of our last days at Rainbow Mountain, the four of us lay a blanket on the grass and had a picnic. As we sat there, I realized that we had become a family. Thankfully, we would remain one for many years. Our picnic was joined by the Rainbow Mountain pooch which came trotting over when he smelled food. We shared our lunch with the dog, and basked in our last moments of freedom and relaxation.

The entire trip was very expensive for that day and age—two thousand dollars per couple for the week. Food, drink and all amenities were included. None of us resented the price or felt exploited. We felt that it was worth every penny, just to have the chance to feel that kind of freedom and equality for several days.

When I close my eyes and think back on it, I can picture it like it was yesterday. I can still hear *Somewhere in Time*. It was like the soundtrack to a movie about the best days of my life. I was the happiest I've ever been at Rainbow Mountain. Remembering it brings tears to my eyes. I couldn't even believe that such a place could exist.

Ten

When the time came to think about packing up and heading home, a somber mood fell over us. We weren't ready to face the reality of returning to the real world with all of its constraints.

"It was so exhilarating being here," I said to Carol, Tommy and John. "I don't want to go home. I really want to stay here!"

"We know! We feel the same way…but what can we do?"

All of us were feeling the same way. If we had been given the option to live the rest of our lives on Rainbow Mountain, we would have done it.

I said, "Well, let's make a plan to come back in a few months. That way, it will be easier to face going home." So, we planned our next trip.

Driving home, we were each lost in our own thoughts and filled with many emotions. I was thrilled to know that Rainbow Mountain existed. Yet, in a way, just knowing it existed made it all the more excruciating to go back into hiding. It made me sad and a little bit angry.

I kept saying to myself, *Enough already! This is ridiculous. We should be able to be ourselves and relax, like we did on Rainbow Mountain.*

Carol and I were eleven years into our relationship by this point in time. Yet, we were still hiding the truth from both our families, some friends, and everyone at work except John. As far as I was concerned, it was wearying, frustrating and just plain wrong.

Of course, societal taboos against same-sex couples was only one of the reasons that Carol and I continued to stay in hiding. The other reason was Carol herself. She wasn't ready or willing to reveal the truth about our relationship.

I was fearless, as I've mentioned. Had it been up to me, I would have been open and out with everyone I knew, and free with public displays of affection. My attitude would have been, *Let's let the chips fall where they may.*

I wanted Carol to be happy and comfortable, so I sublimated my own nature. As long as I knew that Carol was terrified of the ramifications of being out, I felt I had to go along with the secrecy plan. For now, we remained close "cousins" in the eyes of most of the people in our lives.

Walking in the door of our apartment, we were in a state of full-blown culture shock. It was as if we had returned home from another country—or planet. Suddenly, I felt like a stranger in my own home. I no longer felt like I belonged there. I had experienced many emotions during my years in hiding with Carol, but this was a first.

Suddenly, the only time I felt free with Carol was inside our apartment. Living on such a high floor, no one could see inside. So, we could keep our shades open and didn't have to hide.

Carol's reentry into our normal life took a real toll on her. She fell into a bit of a depression and went even further into the closet. She was more reticent than ever to hold hands in front of anyone. And, she went out of her way to avoid eye contact with me. She worried that someone might notice the love we had for each other.

Even in this day and age, with all the progress the LGBTQ+ community has made in terms of equality, there are elderly gay couples who remain in the closet. Their feeling is, "We'd rather be closeted than subject ourselves to discrimination." They know that homophobia is a very real thing, even now.

"I confided in one of the women in my assisted living," said an elderly gay man in a YouTube video, "and she went around the facility and told everyone I was gay. Now, at mealtimes, the very people I used to sit and eat with are saying things to me like, 'Get out of here, faggot!'"

Even though it was hard to be totally free on Rainbow Mountain and then have to return home to a sort of bondage, Carol and I were comforted by our memories of our time there. We never forgot that there was at least one place on earth where things had already changed.

When it was time to take our return trip to Rainbow Mountain, none of us could afford to stay longer than three days. That was long enough. Even in the first ten minutes, hope began to reignite inside us. We felt like we had traveled in a time capsule to the future, to a world we had only dreamed of in our imaginations.

Eleven

Carol and I planned a trip to the Catskills to go skiing. It would be the first time for both of us, and we were very excited. We went out and bought all the cute ski clothing we could find—jackets, pants, shoes and ski boots with soft, warm lining which we loved. (We were planning to rent our skis.)

We had always talked about learning to ski but now we were really going to become skiers. We were both homebodies and spent a lot of time indoors, so we thought that skiing would do us good. We were looking forward to the exhilaration of skiing in the cold, crisp mountain air.

We checked into the ski lodge where we had reservations and made arrangements for ski lessons. Before we knew it, we were on our skis and ready to embrace the experience. As I got off the ski lift and started heading down the mountain, I quickly gained such speed that I lost control of my skis. I flipped up in the air, my poles took flight, and I landed on my tush—and kept on going.

As I went sliding down the mountain, I slid right past Carol. She had fallen off the ski lift, losing one shoe and boot as she tumbled down. She was calling out to me. I had gained such velocity going downhill on my backside, it was impossible for me to stop. I was headed down the mountain whether I liked it or not.

When I reached the bottom, I turned around and, using my poles, hobbled back uphill to her. My tailbone was so sore, it was a miracle I could walk at all.

As I reached her, she said, "You passed me right by!" She couldn't believe I could have seen her there and not stopped.

"What do you mean? I was flying by on my ass! I couldn't stop."

We started laughing—but our laughter was cut short when we realized we had stayed out too long. Carol's hands were really hurting. When she removed her gloves, we could see that they had turned bright red. We thought that she must have gotten frostbite. This was not the first time Carol's hands had turned red and started hurting when she got cold.

Back inside the lodge, we tried to warm up beside the fire. Carol's hands were turning purple and then red again. Meanwhile, my tailbone was sore, but not too bad. I was more worried about Carol than myself.

"I wonder why warming up by the fire isn't helping your hands that much," I said.

She kept rubbing her hands together. Eventually she warmed up and her hands returned to their normal color. For the remainder of our three-day skiing trip, we stayed in the lodge. For obvious reasons, we were too afraid to get back on our skis. And we also thought we'd better stay where it was warm since Carol seemed to have frostbite.

Once we got home from our trip, Carol's hands were fine—until she found herself cold again. This time it was from the air conditioning at work. Once again, her hands turned red and purple and then they turned black. The black color was a brand-new development and it scared us both. At first, we thought it might have been a holdover from the frostbite.

"Can frostbite stay in your system and come back?" we asked each other.

This went on for a few months after our trip to the Catskills. Carol's feet were reacting to the cold in the same way. They turned from white to blue, based upon the temperature. We realized that we had better make an appointment with the doctor.

"It looks like Raynaud's disease," the doctor told Carol after the examination.

"What's that? We've never heard of it," we said.

"It's a vascular disease that causes certain areas of your body, like your fingers and toes, to feel numb and cold in response to cold temperatures and stress. In Raynaud's, smaller arteries that supply blood to your skin narrow, limiting blood supply to the affected areas. It mostly affects the extremities, even the ears."

That would turn out to be true. Later in life, Carol would end up having trouble with her toes and the tips of her ears.

"How do we treat it?" we asked.

"Well, the thing is, there are two types of Raynaud's disease— primary and secondary. Secondary is the rarer of the two forms. It's more serious because it is caused by an underlying problem. For now, we have no reason to believe there's an underlying problem, so there is no treatment. It might help if you move to a warmer climate. And it will definitely help if you keep your feet covered and wear gloves on your hands when you're cold...even indoors."

Carol had been promoted to operations manager at work. So, she now split her time between the air-conditioned office and the air-conditioned store. One winter evening, as she got into her car and began to make her way home, her car got stuck in the snow.

While Carol was waiting for roadside assistance to arrive, she got out of her car to clear the snow off the windshield. When she got back in the car, she had to wait in the cold. As she sat there, she got more and more chilled. By the time the roadside assistance guy arrived, got the car unstuck, and got Carol back on the road, she was freezing.

When she finally got home and walked in the door, she was shivering. She was frozen to the bone. Her hands were bluish-black and her feet too. I ran a very warm bath for her. Even in the bath, she kept shivering. It was very painful for her and frightening for us both. I sat on the side of the tub as she slowly thawed. Eventually she warmed up—but we were both shaken by the experience.

We returned to the doctor a second time. He said, "Unless other symptoms develop to indicate that an underlying problem is causing the Raynaud's, there is nothing that can be done in terms of treatment. It will always be this way. Frostbite may have triggered the Raynaud's, but you're stuck with it. There's no way to reverse it. Warmer weather would certainly help."

As far as the doctor knew, I was a concerned cousin of Carol's, and we were very close. That's how it was done in our community. You never even told your doctor that you were lesbian or gay. You kept your mouth shut out of fear of being outed.

Gays and lesbians always run the risk that a doctor might refuse to treat them. The one exception to this would be if a man went specifically to a gay clinic. Then, of course, the doctors working there would know that the patients were gay.

At the same time that Carol's Raynaud's Syndrome was getting worse, Tommy and John happened to be in Florida. They were there visiting friends who lived in a condo in North Fort Myers.

"Why don't you come down and see us?" they said. "Get out of New York for a while."

"Okay," we told them, "we'll come visit. Carol could use some time in the warm weather."

Even though the doctor had suggested that Carol's symptoms might improve in a warmer climate, we hadn't given any serious thought to leaving New York. We had spent our entire lives there, our families lived there, and it was our home. We couldn't even *imagine* ourselves living outside New York. But a vacation sounded good.

We easily got time off work from Korvettes, thanks to the fact that we'd been working there for so long. We went to Florida for a week, and stayed in a hotel in Fort Myers. After getting settled, we got in the car and headed over to see Tommy and John. As we drove, we took in the town.

Right away, we were struck by how quiet and serene it seemed. We also noticed that everyone on the streets seemed to have blue eyes and blonde hair, except for the occasional pockets of African Americans we passed by.

As New Yorkers, it was hard to fathom that such segregation still existed. We were a little put off by it. Lee County—where Fort Myers is located—is named after General Lee and is very southern. There is even a photo of General Lee in full uniform hanging in the meeting room of the County Commission. Florida is a smorgasbord, with certain areas being more northern in their culture and some being more southern.

We loved the beauty of Fort Myers, with its unpaved roads and laid-back lifestyle. It was so suburban, it didn't even feel like Florida. To me, Florida was urban Miami, with all of its wonderful diversity and the food, culture and music that go along with it.

Tommy and John's social calendar was mostly devoted to spending time with the friends they had gone there to see. When they could slip away, they showed us around town, we went out to eat, and we went to the beach together.

The climate was mild and stayed warm most of the year. Even in the wintertime, it never got nearly as cold as New York. While we were there, I couldn't help but notice that Carol was feeling better—much better, in fact. The only time her hands were getting cold and turning colors was when we spent too long in air-conditioned places.

Back in our apartment after our trip, we said to each other, "I feel so sad being home. It was so nice to be in a warm place! I even felt comfortable and at home there."

When we heard ourselves saying that a place other than New York felt like home, we were stunned. We couldn't believe our own words. And yet, we were happy to have found a place other than home where we believed we could feel at home. We had both come to the sad conclusion that if we ever wanted Carol to feel better, we were going to have to leave New York.

That was as far as we took it at that time. We returned to our usual routines. Yet, just beneath the surface of our daily lives, we could hear in the distance the ticking of a clock. It was only a matter of time.

Twelve

I was working at the Young Men's & Young Women's Hebrew Association (YMYWHA) of Greater Flushing, New York. They served everyone, not only the Jewish population, but the majority of the people there were Jewish.

The organization employed many social workers. Their mission was to serve the community. They offered various services, including daycare, after-school programs, and camp. They also had many offerings geared towards adults and seniors, including seminars where they brought in speakers.

This is where I would learn about my Jewish culture. I learned about the Jewish holidays like Rosh Hashana and Yom Kippur, and how to celebrate them. Next door to the YMYWHA was a building dedicated to serving survivors of the Holocaust. This broadened my knowledge of Jewish history, as well. I thought it was wonderful that all these Holocaust survivors had a dedicated place to live. I loved going over there and hearing their amazing stories.

Their building was connected to the YMYWHA center by a door. On the other side of their building was an organization that served them lunch. We provided all sorts of services for the survivors. Every Wednesday, we presented a show for them in the auditorium, and served cake and coffee.

My job at the YMYWHA changed my life by making me more intuitively attuned to people. Any time we had a staff meeting, it was like a therapy session. There were always social workers in the meeting, and all the topics centered around people. I was the only one working there who didn't have a degree, but I was treated very well and included in everything. It was a wonderful job and the place felt more like a home than a workplace.

Society was still very conservative back then. This was obvious at the YMYWHA where everything was very family oriented. Even though the Y was conservative, I felt unafraid and unconcerned with people finding out that I was a lesbian. I started coming out to fellow LGBTQ+ people at work and made some new friends.

One day, I was talking with a colleague named Diane and she said, "My girlfriend, Nancy and I..." She went on to tell me a story about some of the different places they went together and some of their vacations.

I knew that when Diane talked about her girlfriend, she meant it literally—not in the way some women use the word to describe a female friend.

The more she talked, the more excited I got. It was important to me for Carol and I to have more friends. *Finally!* I said to myself. *A woman friend who is also a lesbian, right here at work! Maybe the four of us could get together and go places.*

I now realized that Diane must have known that Carol and I were actually romantic partners—not just friends or cousins. That was what made her feel comfortable telling me about Nancy.

Once Diane came out to me, it opened up Carol and me to other friends. I went home and said to Carol, "Well, Diane came out to me today! I am so excited because now we can have some women friends like us."

"Oh, that would be great!" said Carol. She was all for it. After all, there was no threat to her privacy because Diane was someone I knew from *my* workplace, not hers.

When it came time for Diane and Nancy to come over for a visit, we decided that we would all go to Rainbow Mountain. That way, we could visit in a place where all four of us were completely relaxed. Since it was wintertime, Carol wore very warm gloves to protect her hands, and off we went. Carol was too excited about the trip to worry much about her condition.

We got adjacent rooms at the resort. We were all looking forward to waking up there the following morning. We were excited about spending time around other people like us. We knew that it was too cold for us to use the pool. But we knew that in the evenings, they would have dancing in the barn.

For the first couple of days, we all had a wonderful time. Then, on the third morning, we looked out our windows to see everything blanketed in white.

Diane and Nancy came running over to our room. Nancy was hysterical. "Oh, no! It snowed!" said Nancy, between sobs.

Diane had told me in advance of the trip, "Nancy can't go very many places. If she feels trapped, she gets scared. So, we tend to stay home a lot."

When we first set out on the trip to Rainbow Mountain, Nancy was relaxed. She felt safe with us and was looking forward to our getaway. Now, she was completely panicked.

"We're stuck here and we'll never be able to get out!" she said, clearly agitated and distressed.

We all tried to comfort her. "No, don't worry…they will clear the roads and we'll be able to leave. You'll see."

Nothing we said had any effect on Nancy. She was inconsolable. Then we coaxed her out into the snow to build snowmen. Before we knew it, she started having fun and calmed down.

Carol couldn't stay outside in the snow for too long because of her Raynaud's. When we got back into our room, it took some time for her hands to warm up. No matter how much pain Carol was in, she never complained. She still engaged in all the activities she could, even if she suffered the consequences. She felt that playing in the snow had been worth it because it took Nancy's mind off her fears.

It was wonderful to be with another female couple. And through them, we met other friends. Up until then, our only gay friends had been Tommy and John. And, while we adored them, they were not women. We craved the company of other lesbian women.

The next LGBTQ+ person I discovered at the Y was an eighteen-year old guy named Anthony who worked for me. He came to the Y as part of the CETA program, a government-sponsored program for people without a job or skills.

These nonskilled workers were provided with jobs in nonprofits like the YMYWHA. The government paid their salaries for about a year. If, after a year, the worker had proven themselves to be a good worker, the company would hire them on a permanent basis. We had four CETA workers at the Y.

One morning when I got to the Y, I found Anthony sleeping on the couch in the office of the center director. He was dressed all in black leather. In that moment, it came to me—he was gay. It was clear that he had not been home the night before. He had obviously slept there. (He cleaned the building on the night shift and had access to all the offices.)

Oh, this is interesting! I said to myself. *Why wouldn't he have gone home?*

I knew that Anthony was living with his brother. I thought that maybe he had been drunk the night before and felt like it would be safer to sleep at the office. He was young and appeared to be floundering in his life. I knew that I needed to help him.

When I woke him up, he was startled. He hadn't realized that it was morning and didn't expect anyone to discover him there.

"The director will be in soon," I said. "You need to get into your street clothes before she finds you here. Hurry up and get home!"

Later that day when he arrived for his shift, he came into my office and we talked. I decided to get right to the point. "Are you gay?" I asked him.

After a moment of hesitation, he admitted, "I think I am." He was unsure at first, and then later, he met a guy named Ron. That brought him certainty.

"I am too," I said.

Tears started rolling down his cheeks. "Thank you so much for talking to me about this," he said, still crying from a combination of relief and gratitude. "I really appreciate it. I can't tell my brother I'm gay. He's so macho. And now, you're the only other gay person I know."

"Don't worry about being gay," I said. "I'll always be here for you if you need somebody to talk to. I know what it's like to be alone and have nobody to talk to about being gay. But you can't do what you did last night. No more sleeping in the director's office."

Anthony would go on to have a healthy, longstanding gay relationship with Ron, and a good life. (Very recently, I tried to reach out to him. When I called, I got a disconnected-number recording. Sadly, I found his obituary online.)

Anthony gave me permission to tell Diane that he was gay. Now there were three of us LGBTQ+ employees at the Y. We all took comfort in knowing we had each other.

Not long afterward, I told Carol that I thought we should have a small New Year's Eve party. Knowing that anyone I invited would be affiliated with my workplace, not hers, she was excited about the idea. We planned the party together, decorated our place, and made the hors d'oeuvres. We made teriyaki chicken wings and antipasto salad. And, we bought New Year's Eve hats and plastic blower horns for everyone to blow at midnight.

We invited Tommy and John, Diane and Nancy, Anthony and his boyfriend, Ron, along with two other female friends of Diane's. There were ten of us in total. We played music, danced, and had the best time. Because everyone at the party was gay, we all felt free to be ourselves in front of each other.

At midnight, we watched the ball drop in Times Square and toasted each other with flutes of champagne. I still have photos of Carol and me in our party hats, dancing to standards by Engelbert Humperdinck, Andy Williams and Barbara Streisand. You can see from the photos how happy we were that night.

It would end up being our last New Year's Eve in New York. The cold, bitter winters were taking their toll on Carol's health.

Thirteen

Carol and I had been making regular vacation trips to Fort Myers. Whenever we went, we stayed in hotels. Then, on one of our trips there, we looked at each other and said, "Why don't we just buy a little vacation house down here? That way, we can save money on hotels."

So, we got ourselves a realtor who started keeping an eye out for us. One day, she took us to see a little one-bedroom condo with a one-car garage in Fort Myers. It had a nice-sized kitchen, one bedroom, one bathroom, and carpeting. Outside was a pretty lanai with yellow flowers. It felt more like a little house than a condo and it was listed for only $23,000.

When we walked into the condo, Carol and I agreed, "It's perfect for us!" So, we went ahead and bought it. For the next three years, we flew down to Florida and stayed in our condo about twice a year or whenever we could get time off work. We also let relatives use the condo for a getaway from time to time.

Since the weather in Florida is mild year-round, we didn't need to be present to do the kind of maintenance necessitated by living in a climate with snow and ice.

Over time, returning to our apartment in New York after our trips to Florida made us both a little melancholy. We would walk in the door of our apartment and wish we were still in Florida. This came as a huge surprise to us native New Yorkers.

We said to each other, "Is it really possible that we actually miss our little Florida condo when we're home in New York? What are we doing?"

We knew that we could never afford to buy a place in New York. And we were all too aware that we needed to live in a warm climate for Carol's health. She felt much better when we were in Florida. Down there, we could control the air conditioning. The climate in our New York apartment was controlled by the building.

"Let's not say anything to anyone about the fact that we're thinking of moving," we agreed. "Let's send out some resumes first and see if at least one of us can get a job there. If one of us can get a job, we can move knowing we'll have money coming in. The other one can figure out their job situation once we get down there."

Both Carol and I started sending out resumes to businesses in the Cape Coral/Fort Myers area, applying for all types of jobs. I applied for jobs at community centers, synagogues, and even the county. We knew that once we got down there, we could always look for another job if we were unhappy. So, we set the bar low for our initial Florida job prospects.

Neither of us was religious. Yet, when we took trips to Fort Myers on vacation, we did attend synagogues—something we never did in New York. I can't account for the fact that we only went to synagogue when we were in Florida. In any event, on one of our Fort Myers trips, we had gone exploring to see what was in the area, and happened upon the Federation of Jewish Philanthropies.

Now that I was job hunting, I reached out to the executive director, Helene. She helped me find a job as an administrator at a synagogue called Temple Beth-el. It was *bashert*—a Yiddish word for destiny.

After twelve years of working at the YMYWHA, everyone there had become like my family. So, I was very sad to leave them. Both Carol and I would both be leaving our actual families in New York, as well.

Once I knew I had my job in Florida, I went home to see my parents. It was time to break the news to them that we were moving to Florida. They already knew that Carol and I were looking for jobs in Florida. And, they knew that Carol was having health problems exacerbated by living in New York.

I was forty at the time I had the conversation with my parents about Carol and me moving away. This conversation reminded me of the conversation I'd had with them at thirty-five, when Carol and I finally came out to our parents. We had been living on our own for ten years by that point, and still separating our bed into two twins whenever our parents came over.

We were always lying to them about everything—what we were doing, who we were spending time with, and where we were going. We couldn't do it anymore.

"We really need to tell our parents," I had said to Carol. "We've spent our entire lives lying and I'm tired of it. We can't live like this anymore. I don't like to lie."

"Okay, I agree. We need to tell them," she said.

"Really?" I said, stunned. "This is huge for you! You're really going to tell your parents?"

"We have to. We're living together and doing everything together. We can't do it anymore. I will tell them. I don't know how they're going to react. I don't know if they will even talk to me anymore."

We had been trying to protect both her parents and mine from the knowledge that we were two women in a romantic relationship with each other. We weren't really even sure they would understand what that meant. We didn't think they had ever met any other lesbians.

Then again, the concept of homosexuality was not completely foreign to Carol's family. She had a gay uncle who lived with his partner. He never tried to hide the fact that they slept in the same bed. No one ever spoke about it, but I figured everyone had to have known.

Whenever we were at Carol's uncle's house, I would think to myself, *Surely Carol's parents must have noticed that there's only one bed here! Why haven't they put two and two together?*

On the day we were to come out to our parents, we steeled our nerves and got in the car. We were still living in Queens and both her parents and mine still lived in the Bronx. So, we drove to the Bronx from Flushing. On the ride there, we were talking about how nervous we were to finally tell them.

Carol dropped me off at my parents, since I didn't drive. The plan was that I would tell them, and then wait for her downstairs in front of my parents' building. It took me back to when we were twenty-five and trying to break the news to them that we planned to move out together.

My parents didn't know I was coming. I figured they would probably be home because it was a Sunday. I walked into my parents' home and found Mom in the kitchen and Dad in the bedroom.

"I need to talk to you about something important," I said.

We all took a seat in the living room and they looked at me expectantly.

"Carol and I are in a relationship. We're together."

As the meaning of my words began to sink in, my mother began to cry. "You mean, I'll never have any grandchildren?"

"Mom, I'm really sorry, but I love Carol and that's the way it is."

I had been thinking that my parents would be upset that they would miss the chance to watch me get married in a traditional wedding. I always felt a little bit sad over it myself. Mom didn't mention her disappointment over the fact that there would be no wedding—only over not having grandchildren.

I felt terrible about that. I knew how much my mother loved children and how much she was looking forward to becoming a grandmother.

"It's okay," said my father, stoic and calm. "As long as you're happy, I'm happy!"

I was surprised by my dad's reaction—and relieved beyond words. Back then, most people did not reveal their homosexuality to their loved ones. I was astounded that Dad took it so well.

Back in the early 1980s when this conversation took place, society was lightyears away from considering homosexuality an acceptable lifestyle. In fact, anyone discovered to be in a same-sex relationship was considered abnormal—sick, even.

I took Dad's mild reaction as proof that, just as I had always suspected, he already knew that Carol and I were more than friends. I had gotten that impression at various points throughout my life.

My mother recovered her composure and agreed with Dad that my happiness was all that mattered. Before I left, they both gave me a hug and a kiss.

On my way out the door, Mom said to me, "If you were with a guy, you would have told me, right?"

"Yes, I would have."

"But you felt like you couldn't tell me?" she asked.

"I was afraid because I didn't think you would understand," I explained.

"I was just upset over never having any grandchildren…"

Neither my brother nor my sister ever got married or had any children. So, they never gave my parents grandchildren either. Heidi did have children, and my parents considered them their grandchildren. Up until my father's death, my parents and Heidi's children remained close.

After I told my parents that Carol and I were a couple, I told my brother, Les, and my sister, Phyllis. I invited the two of them over to our place, and Carol and I told them together.

Like my dad, Les was happy for me. And like Dad, he had always had a feeling that there was something going on with me.

"I've always loved Carol," he told me. "And I knew you were really good friends. I had a feeling something might be going on, but I didn't know what it was, exactly."

Just like Les had, Phyllis told me, "It's absolutely fine. I feel good that you're happy. And anyway, Carol is already part of the family."

I knew that in her heart of hearts, Phyllis was hurt and resentful. She had apparently been living in Queens at the same time as Carol and I, and attending a local college. We were not in touch at the time. (These days, we maintain a relationship and speak from time to time.)

Phyllis really needed me during the early period of her life. She always felt overlooked at home, and felt that Heidi had replaced her as the baby of the family. Being close with me would have really helped her.

I believe that my relationship with Carol, and the energy it took to protect it from scrutiny and keep our secret, led to me becoming distant from my siblings. It all stemmed from the ability to compartmentalize that I developed early in my life. I became an expert at tucking away my painful feelings over having to keep my secret. Sadly, that sometimes meant that some of my loved ones got put out of my mind along with the painful feelings.

I think the fact that I had kept my distance was hurtful to both of my siblings, and Heidi as well. I now realize that I wasn't there for them during the years when they really needed me. I was thinking of myself and what I wanted, and not of them. But there's nothing I can do about that now.

I would go back and change it if I could, but we can't turn back the hands of time. All we can do is continue to move forward and try to do better. I made Carol my whole word. Interestingly, I never disconnected from my parents. Our bond was always rock solid.

When I disconnected from my siblings to focus on Carol, I think it probably stung Heidi even more than Phyllis. Heidi and I were closer than I had been with my own sister.

I was in my early thirties when Heidi and I first reconnected. She was living in a group home for teenagers in Queens and attending college locally. Now that she was living in the group home, Heidi was closer to my parents' home. So, she was able to get over there for holidays. Even after all my family put her through, Heidi still joined our family to celebrate the holidays. So, I got to see her then.

When Heidi left that group home and got her own apartment when she was eighteen, I visited her there.

One night, I got a disturbing call from Heidi. "Can you come over? I'm sitting on the windowsill in my apartment and I think I might jump!"

When I got to her place, I went inside and found her still sitting on the windowsill. She was looking out at the cemetery across the street. I walked over to her and put my arms around her—and she let me. She needed and wanted my attention, and I completely understood.

We hugged and kissed and I told her, "I love you so much, Heidi!"

"I love you, too, Arlene! And you need to know…I'm not good. I need help."

"Tell me," I said, "what do you need?"

"I need to go to the doctor. I'm bulimic. I throw up my food."

I slept over at her place that night. I wanted to make sure she didn't wake up distressed and decide to end it all.

In the morning, Heidi said, "I'm okay now, Arlene. You can go."

I will never know whether or not it was seeing me that made Heidi change her mind about taking her life. I was just glad that she had stabilized overnight.

I told her that I was going to make an appointment for her with a doctor and return later that week to take her to the appointment.

When Heidi and I walked into the doctor's office, her palms and her feet were orange from eating so many carrots. My heart really went out to her.

I came out to Heidi right around the same time I told everyone else about Carol and me. Heidi told me that she loved Carol. I knew that she probably felt the same way that Phyllis did—that I had put Carol before everyone else. It was true.

Mom, dad and I just a babe in the Bronx, New York 1947

Dad, me & mom in the Bronx @ Grandma Libby & Grandpa Abe's
house 1949

Just me

Grandma Libby & Grandpa Abe in the Bronx on Coster Street

Me & my brother Les on Vyse Ave. In the Bronx 1951

Arlene Goldberg

Carol at home on Elder Ave. In the Bronx

Me, Les & my sister Phyllis in a lot in the Bronx 1956

Me, my brother & sister on Vyse Avenue in the Bronx 1958

Me & Carol both 14 years old @ a YM-YWCA convention
in Connecticut in 1961

Friends got together in Castle Hill Projects in 1962. We were both
15 years old (me bottom right corner/Carol top left corner)

Both of us graduate from J.H.S. 101 in the Bronx in 1962
(Carol in the front/me in the back)

Me & Carol in Castle Hill Projects in the Bronx in 1967
both 20 years old

Our vacation Hideaway in P-Town, Mass in 1968

Leaving for our trip to Europe @ Laguardia airport in Queens,
New York in 1969

At home with my sister

Thankfully we discover Rainbow Mountain Resort in the
Poconos, New Jersey

Tommy & John join us on our Rainbow Mountain vacation

Me, Tommy & Carol at Rainbow Mountain

Carol & I freely showing our love at Rainbow Mountain

Feeling free at Rainbow Mountain

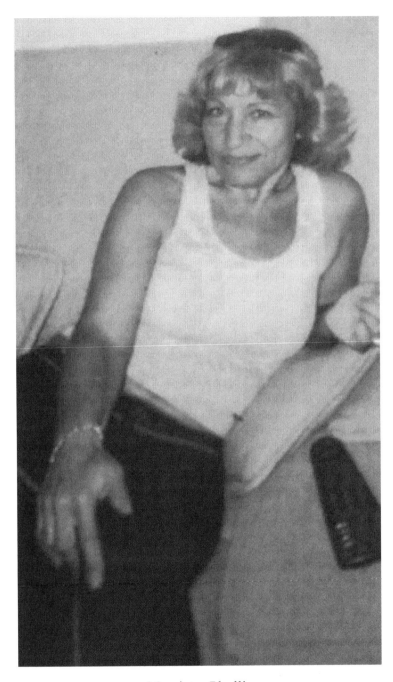

My sister Phyllis

Heidi, dad, mom, Phyllis, Les & I in a family photo (left to right)

A great trio mom, me & Aunt Rhoda (mom's sister)

P-Town once more...Carol and I

Best friends on a P-Town vacation..freedom once more. (left front to back) Carol, Tommy & John (right front to back) me, Barbara & Shelly

At home with me, mom & Carol in the Bronx

Dear Carol (heart)

Disneyworld vacation- me & Carol

John, me, Carol & Tommy...dear friends

Our first owned home ever in Fort Myers, Florida

Carol, Mikey & I in our new home.

We two just relaxing at home

Caribbean cruise with my love

Dressed for the evening on our Caribbean vacation

My darling dad and I dancing

St. Petersburg, Florida Pride event

Washington D.C. Pride Parade & demonstration

Applying for our marriage license in 2011 in New York

Waiting outside the Queens courthouse in New York to get married on
October 21, 2011

Carol placed the wedding band on my finger sealing our marriage

Barbara & Shelly had their wedding the same day with us

Two (2) joyful couples ....married at last!!!

Shelly, Barbara, Carol & I in Denver Co.

Fundraising Cruise for Visuality in Fort Myers...It was flapper fun!!

Our final vacation together....San Francisco in 2013

Arlene Goldberg

Mom & Dad of my heart....

Our chosen family: Carol, Tommy, John, me, Barbara & Shelly in
New York City in 2011.

Dear Carol with our new puppy Lacey in 2013

WE CAN'T WAIT ANY LONGER!

Attorney General Bondi wants to delay this summer's landmark marriage rulings. But every single day that the freedom to marry is delayed, Floridians like Arlene Goldberg - whose wife Carol passed away this year before Florida respected their marriage - are harmed.

 Equality Florida

GetEngaged.org

Q + A

ARLENE'S STORY

Arlene Goldberg and Carol Goldwasser had been inseparable since they were teenagers. They became a couple at the age of 20, and had been together for 47 years. They married in New York when that state permitted same sex marriage several years ago.

On March 13, 2014, the very day that the ACLU of Florida announced its lawsuit challenging Florida's marriage ban, Carol passed away after a long illness. Because of Florida's discriminatory marriage ban, the grieving Arlene was treated like a legal stranger to the person she loved and shared a life with for half a century.

Arlene contacted the ACLU of Florida and was added to the case as a plaintiff. When the judge issued his ruling, he stayed it except for one part: he ordered the Florida Surgeon General to issue a corrected death certificate to reflect Carol's marriage to Arlene, making Arlene the first Floridian to have her marriage to a partner of the same sex recognized by a Florida state agency.

Arlene (L) and Carol (R)

ACLU: After being together for so long, why was it important to you and Carol to get legally married?

ARLENE: Originally, we felt we didn't need a piece of paper to ensure our relationship would survive because it was about love. Carol knew she was ill and didn't know where her illness would take her so she wanted to ensure I would be eligible to receive her social security benefits should she pass away.

ACLU: The ACLU's marriage lawsuit was filed during what must've been the hardest week of your life. What did it feel like to have your marriage to Carol treated as if it didn't exist?

ARLENE: It was hurtful, especially when Carol was listed as "single - never married", on her death certificate, and that I was her "informant."

ACLU: Why did you decide to reach out to the ACLU for help?

ARLENE: I read the ACLU had filed a lawsuit to have eight same sex couples' marriages outside of Florida recognized in Florida and I knew I would encounter roadblocks trying to secure Carol's benefits. I called and asked if the ACLU could add my case to the existing lawsuit.

ACLU: What would Carol say about the fact that the story of your relationship helped win marriage equality in Florida?

ARLENE: I think Carol would be proud that marriage equality in Florida was helped to become a reality because of our love and now her legacy.

Fourteen

On the day that Carol and I agreed to tell our parents about us, I told mine first and then went downstairs to wait for her. While I was waiting, I was anxious and worried. Both Carol and I feared that her parents might shun her once they found out about us. We knew how devastated they had been when we moved out—and that was nothing compared to this news!

A few days before Carol came out to her parents, she decided to speak to her sister, who was still living at home.

"I'm going to tell Arline first," Carol said. "I need backup when I tell my parents!"

When Carol and Arline were young, they had a close relationship, and they would for most of their lives. There was an eleven-year age difference between them. So, they didn't spend that much time together, but they were close. (Later in life, a situation would arise where Carol and I objected to a major life choice Arline was making. That would end up causing a serious rift between Arline and us—and sadly, the rift endures to this day.)

Arline had known me since she was very young. She had grown up with me around. When Carol explained to Arline that we were in a relationship, and we were a couple, Arline took the news very well.

"I love you both so much," she told Carol, "there is nothing you could do that would make me feel badly about you."

Carol and I met up after she had broken the news to her parents. She said, "I told my parents that we were in a relationship and my father said to me, 'What do you mean?' And I said, 'What do you mean, what do I mean?' Then he turned and looked at my sister who already knew because I told her first…"

As I said earlier, Carol's mother's brother was in a gay relationship. So, it wasn't like Carol's parents had never had exposure to homosexuals before. And yet, her father could not seem to understand how his own daughter could be gay.

Carol went on, "Arline explained to them, 'Dad, Carol and Arlene are in a *relationship*. They're a couple!'"

Carol's mom started to cry. "You're not going to have a wedding? You're not going to give us grandchildren?"

Once her mother had a few minutes to digest the news, she said, "Are you going to be happy? Are you happy now?"

"I'm fine, Mom! I'm very happy!" said Carol.

Carol's father just kept repeating, "I don't understand this. It is unacceptable!" Being so old-world, he couldn't wrap his brain around our lifestyle.

"Well, this is the way it is," Carol explained to her father. "Arlene and I are already together."

Her parents' reaction, and especially her father's, was very hard on Carol. She had enjoyed an extremely close relationship with them for her entire life up until then. Now things were suddenly very strained between them. The fact that Carol's parents hadn't outright shunned her was cold comfort.

As Carol left her parents' apartment that day, she was crying, her Mom was crying, and her dad was very upset. Carol was still teary-eyed when she came to tell me what had happened. We both felt terrible. She had known that my parents would take the news better than hers. Still, she had hoped things with her parents would go better than they did.

When I saw Carol's parents a few days later, they conducted themselves as they always had with me. I felt like they should have acknowledged that they knew about Carol and me—as my parents had done. They could have broken the ice by saying something along the lines of, "Carol told us about the two of you." And then they could have talked about how they felt about the news.

Instead, they completely sidestepped the fact that Carol had ever brought up the subject to them. They swept it right under the rug and carried on as usual. They seemed utterly unable to absorb the reality. It was too much for them to take in.

Even though Carol had now come out to her parents and her sister, she remained in the closet at her new job in Florida. There were only a few people at Carol's workplace who knew the truth about us.

I, on the other hand, had no qualms about telling people at my job. To some extent, it was Carol's declining health that led to me telling people at work. I needed to be able to explain my absences from work.

In 2006, when we were both fifty-nine years old, Carol started to develop high fevers in the morning. She would wake up around 5:00 a.m., burning up. The fever was usually accompanied by terrible nausea and sometimes loose stools. She would run into the bathroom to be sick, and then get back into bed.

I would take her temperature, which was often as high as 104 or 105. I would use every home remedy I could think of, trying to get her fever down. I was usually able to lower her fever, but it would take about an hour and a half.

Carol often remained nauseous throughout the course of the day. It was horrible. This went on for six months. We didn't go to the doctor right away. We both felt that the problem couldn't be too urgent if I was able to bring Carol's fevers down with home remedies. It was obvious to us both that Carol had stomach problems but, other than that, she seemed okay.

The doctor examined Carol but couldn't come up with a diagnosis. He did blood tests on her and *still* couldn't come up with a diagnosis. Then one workday morning, Carol got up and had such a high fever, she knew that there was no way she could go in to work. She was extremely distraught because she was working on a special bridge project at work that day in her capacity as toll facilities director.

"This is affecting your life so badly, we really have to find out what's going on!" I said. "We can't keep doing this!"

So, we went back to the doctor. This time, he ordered a blood test to check for autoimmune disorders. The test came back positive.

"Well," the doctor said to Carol, "it looks like you do have an autoimmune disease. But I don't know which one it is."

I couldn't believe my ears. "What do you mean you don't know which one it is? Can't this test tell you that?"

"No, it can't. All it can tell us is that Carol has some kind of autoimmune disease."

As soon as I found out that Carol had an autoimmune disease of some kind, I spent a lot of time on the internet, researching. I had a feeling that she might have scleroderma. Her symptoms seemed to match the symptoms listed for that disease. Before I started researching autoimmune diseases, neither Carol nor I had ever heard of scleroderma so we didn't know anything about the disease.

(Autoimmune diseases are hereditary. In Carol's situation, her mother's parents were first cousins. The descendants of first cousins often have medical issues. In fact, Carol's sister has lupus, an autoimmune disease. So, Carol wasn't the only child with autoimmune problems.)

It turned out that there was no further testing that could be done by this internist/infectious diseases doctor. The ANA test—the one he had already ordered—was the only test he could order.

So, I said to Carol, "We have to find out what's going on. We're going to Baltimore to the scleroderma clinic at Johns Hopkins."

By now, Carol was frantic. "It's so scary to not know what's wrong with me!"

It was very unsettling and nerve-wracking for us both to know that there was something wrong with her but not have a name for the disease.

"Don't worry," I said, "we're going to get to the bottom of this."

By now, Carol was also having trouble with her feet. The skin on the bottom of her feet was thinning, the cushiony pads were disappearing, and walking was becoming more difficult for her. She could feel the bones in her feet when she walked.

When I called Johns Hopkins and spoke to someone in the scleroderma clinic, I was told that Carol's symptoms sounded like they might be indicative of scleroderma. This assessment matched what I had suspected myself after doing my research. So, it rang true to me.

As I came to learn about scleroderma, I would say to myself, *All that internalized denial of her true self had to come out, one way or another. I'll bet that's what this illness is all about.*

"Why don't you come up to Baltimore and get evaluated in our scleroderma clinic?" they said.

Carol was at the point where she could no longer go to work anyway, so this plan seemed like our only option. She asked for a medical leave from work and it was immediately granted. Everyone at her workplace could see that she was really feeling unwell.

We made an appointment for her at Johns Hopkins. Unfortunately, they couldn't see her for two or three weeks. Thankfully, it was summertime. Had it been winter, Carol could not have made the trip to Baltimore. The cold weather would have triggered her Raynaud's Syndrome.

Fifteen

For our trip to Baltimore, Carol wore thick sneakers and pads in her shoes. (They had been given to her by the doctor.) The pads helped cushion her feet so that walking wasn't as painful. Before Carol had gotten sick, she was a regular Imelda Marcos when it came to shoes. It was so sad to see her lose the ability to wear all of her beautiful shoes.

When the time came, we flew up to Baltimore and checked into a hotel as cousins. We got a room with only one bed. Thankfully, the front desk staff didn't look at us sideways. I'm sure that female cousins sharing a bed didn't seem that out of the ordinary.

Very early the next day, I took Carol to her appointment at the scleroderma clinic at Johns Hopkins. I already knew from my own research that scleroderma is a vascular disease, one that literally eats up a person's body. All the stress that accumulated over the years from denying and hiding her true self had no doubt exacerbated Carol's illness and sped up her decline.

We would also discover that there are two types of scleroderma. One is systemic and affects the internal organs. The other affects the patient's skin. It causes the skin to become stretched taut. As we sat in the waiting room of the clinic, waiting to see the doctor, we saw a couple of people whose skin was very taut. Everyone else looked fine— probably an indication that they had the type of scleroderma that affects the internal organs.

When Carol was called in to see Dr. Hummer, the female doctor, she asked if I could come with her into the exam room. The doctor didn't object. She was a slight woman in her forties and very caring. She also seemed a little bit sad.

I thought to myself, *It's probably the specialty she's in that's making her sad. Most of these cases don't have happy endings.*

After the exam, Dr. Hummer told us, "I need to order some tests so we can find out exactly what's going on here. I'm going to order a CT-scan, an MRI and some blood tests."

The doctor told us that it was going to take a couple of days to have all the tests done and get the results. When we planned our trip, we had allowed ourselves three or four days at Johns Hopkins, so this didn't come as any surprise.

As I said, from the time I first spoke to the scleroderma clinic at Johns Hopkins, I suspected that Carol was going to get a scleroderma diagnosis. Carol also knew that there was a good chance of that. The tests would confirm not only whether or not Carol did indeed have scleroderma, but also which type.

We were told to take a seat in the waiting room while they scheduled some tests for Carol. Before they sent us to the waiting room, they also drew her blood. Some of her blood would be used for the lab tests and the remainder would be kept in a blood bank for research purposes.

While we waited, we were both really scared. We had a feeling that the outcome would be exactly what we feared. From the little we already knew about the disease, we knew that a scleroderma diagnosis was very bad news.

Later that day, Carol was given a full-body MRI at Johns Hopkins. As she went into the room where the MRI was being done, I had to stay behind. Since Carol was having trouble with her feet, she was also sent to the ultrasound department for a scan.

I was happy to be allowed in the room with Carol while the ultrasound was being done. They did an ultrasound of her legs so they could track the blood flow to her feet. Carol was told as the ultrasound was being administered that there was very little blood flow getting to her feet because the veins were colluded (turning hard).

When Carol heard this, she started to cry, saying, "What's going to happen to my feet?"

The ultrasound technician said, "We're going to see if we can get the blood flowing to your feet. We may be able to do this surgically by taking a vein from somewhere else in your body and putting it down by your ankle."

Carol and I knew that all the test results would be going to Dr. Hummer and that she would go over everything with us.

I kept thinking to myself, *Scleroderma is deadly and there's no cure for it. If that's what she has, we're in for a really bad time.*

The phone conversation I initially had with the scleroderma clinic kept returning to my memory. When they told me that Carol's symptoms sounded indicative of scleroderma, I had asked about the life expectancy of scleroderma patients. I was told that it depended upon the type of scleroderma. I was also told that with the systemic type, it was about five years from diagnosis. It varies from person to person.

When I did my own research and read about the disease, I knew that Carol wouldn't have long to live, and that her remaining years would be a constant battle. The bad ultrasound, showing lack of blood flow to Carol's feet, confirmed everything I already suspected.

As we headed back toward the hotel that evening, I thought to myself, *From here on in, nothing that happens with Carol's health is going to surprise me. I know where this is headed.*

Our hotel was located on the water in a very picturesque area. So, we decided to stop and relax over a nice dinner on the bay before going up to our room.

Over dinner, we talked. "I'm more concerned about your feet than anything else," I said. "If the blood's not going to your feet, what will happen to them? You could end up not being able to walk at all!"

"You're right!" she agreed. "I don't know what to do. I guess we'll have to wait and see what the doctor says and take it from there. We're right where we need to be, at Johns Hopkins. I think I'll be fine, now that we're here."

Carol seemed to be telling herself that whatever was wrong with her, John's Hopkins would be able to take care of it.

I knew better. As I said, I already knew the trajectory that scleroderma followed, and the life expectancy that went along with it. I didn't say anything. I didn't have the heart to dash her hopes.

I figured, *If the doctor doesn't set her straight, I'm not going to. She's not a very resilient person and she'd take it really hard.*

Throughout her entire medical ordeal, Carol kept her fears and worries mostly to herself and never complained. She always remained hopeful—and used denial as a means to cope. She never let herself accept the grimness of her medical situation. I think she wanted to protect not only herself from the terrible reality of scleroderma but me too.

This left me in a strange position. I knew and accepted the harsh realities of Carol's illness. Those realities made me very sad. I was frustrated because I couldn't discuss the situation with Carol. She obviously didn't want to face the truth, and I didn't want to upset her further by bringing it up.

As we got into bed at the hotel that night, we didn't yet have confirmation of Carol's diagnosis. But in my heart, I already knew what the morning would bring. And I'm sure on some deep level, Carol did too.

Sixteen

Carol came by her tendencies for denial honestly. As you know by now, her family never dealt with anything. They just looked the other way when something was upsetting or unpleasant, and kept quiet about it.

I am a realist. I kept hoping that my realism might rub off on Carol. In all the years we were together, it never did. Maybe having me as the realist, the one who did research, allowed her the luxury of sticking her head in the sand. Maybe she figured that I would tell her anything she really needed to know. I do know for sure that she took comfort in knowing I would stick by her side and take care of her, no matter what.

The morning after all the testing, we headed down to the hotel buffet for breakfast before meeting with the doctor for the results. After breakfast, sitting in the doctor's waiting room at the hospital, I suddenly got really nervous.

I said to myself, *Well, this is the moment of truth! I wonder if the doctor will tell us how long Carol's likely to live.*

I had so many thoughts in my head—but I didn't feel that I could share them with Carol. She wasn't as strong, or as able to handle adversity.

When Dr. Hummer called us in, she said, "I'm sorry to tell you this but Carol has systemic scleroderma."

Carol finally had a definitive diagnosis. We both started crying.

"There is no cure. So, all we can do," she explained, "is monitor the disease and do our best to keep it from progressing beyond the stage it's at."

Of course, the disease's progression was going to continue, regardless of the monitoring.

The doctor continued, "…It's going to affect the vascular system throughout your whole body, Carol."

"What does that mean?" I asked.

"Well, it will affect her stomach…"

"It is already affecting it!" I said. "Carol's been vomiting and having trouble going to the bathroom."

"And it will affect muscles everywhere in the body," continued the doctor. "It will weaken your muscles and harden all your organs."

If Dr. Hummer gave us a life expectancy prognosis, I never heard it. But I knew that systemic scleroderma was a death sentence because I had researched it in advance of the appointment.

"You'll need to see a rheumatologist," said Dr. Hummer. "They handle auto-immune diseases. And then you'll return here in six months or a year for further testing, so we can see how far it has progressed."

I reminded the doctor that Carol had Raynaud's and was sensitive to the cold. So, we would have to wait until the summer to return. (Raynaud's can either be a primary disease, meaning a standalone disease, or it can be secondary to scleroderma. We now knew that Carol's Raynaud's was secondary to scleroderma.)

"You'll have to see specialists for your various organs as they begin to be affected by the scleroderma," continued Dr. Hummer.

"So, you mean that every time Carol has an issue, she'll have to see a doctor related to that part of the body?"

"That's right. So, be sure to get established with a rheumatologist," said the doctor in closing, "and as symptoms appear with other organs, that's the time to go see those specialists."

When I thought about scleroderma, it seemed like science fiction, with all the organs turning hard and shutting down.

As we left Dr. Hummer's office at 10:00 a.m., with this hideous news hanging over our heads, we were reminded to make another appointment a year from then.

I couldn't help but say to myself, *What's the point of coming back here? It won't make any difference. There's nothing they can do except monitor the disease.*

Carol didn't share with me her thoughts or feelings as we were leaving the doctor's office. Whenever I brought up the subject, she always said, "We'll just go see all the doctors and figure out how we can handle this."

If I had been the one diagnosed, I would have told Carol how pointless it seemed to go back for an annual follow-up. And, I would have talked about how ridiculous it seemed to go to a different specialist each time a symptom arose in a body part.

I can only imagine how lonely she must have felt, keeping all her feelings about scleroderma bottled up. She did go into an online scleroderma chat room and share her thoughts, feelings and fears. I found out about that only after she died. Around me, she kept up a cheerful, hopeful front. I knew that she was doing this out of love. She didn't want to worry me. The truth was, I would have felt ten times more reassured by honest, in-depth conversations.

In any case, I didn't let her reticence to discuss it distance me. I always made sure to stay close to her emotionally. We returned home that same day. On the plane, I tried to talk to Carol about her diagnosis and what the doctor had just told us.

It was so strange to realize that Carol had just received what was essentially a death sentence. You couldn't tell to look at her. Since she didn't have the skin-pulling type of scleroderma, there were no outward signs of her diagnosis. None of our friends knew what was going on.

As we arrived home, I was saying to myself, *We have a lot of work to do now. We have to remain strong and at least see if there's any chance we can beat it.*

We told Tommy and John about Carol's scleroderma diagnosis, but Carol didn't want to discuss it with anyone. She wanted to believe she would get better, and I needed to hope right along with her. There was always an off chance that a miracle would come our way.

I also decided not to push for too much conversation with Carol about her illness. I knew that talking too much about what was happening made it more real for her. I wanted her to have what she needed. Denial seemed to be the thing she needed in order to deal with her reality.

Just as Carol's parents stuck their heads in the sand over the news of her being romantically involved with me, they were in denial about the gravity of her illness. They knew we had gone to Johns Hopkins and they knew about Carol's scleroderma diagnosis. But they weren't the type to research it or dig too deeply into the details.

I don't recall Carol's parents ever asking her whether or not her illness was deadly. And I'm sure if they *did* ask, Carol would have followed the unspoken family rule of painting a rosy picture of the situation. Of course, that picture had little to do with the reality.

That's exactly what Carol did with me. She did her best to avoid the truth about her prognosis—but I was always painfully aware of it. I was with her at the doctor's appointments and I knew the truth.

When she was diagnosed, Carol and I talked about how we wanted to proceed in terms of our lifestyle.

"I don't want to talk about my illness with people. They'll start seeing me as sick," said Carol. "People look at you differently when you're really sick. And I don't want to let scleroderma stop us from traveling or doing whatever we want to do."

I was totally on board with that plan. But, when we traveled, we needed to stay near a hospital at all times. So, going to places like Rainbow Mountain was out.

On the other hand, I was not on board with keeping the news about Carol's illness a secret. I decided that I would tell a handful of our closest friends. I felt that it was important for them to know. I asked them all to be discreet and not mention to Carol that they knew. They all agreed. I never told Carol what I had done because I wanted to protect her from upset.

I am a very open person by nature and I really hate keeping secrets—but we had done it our entire lives. If Carol had also been open, we would never have needed to keep any secrets. I honored her wishes on things she wanted to keep quiet about as much as I could manage. There were certain things I felt I simply needed to speak up about.

Secret keeping would remain an unfortunate and unwanted part of my life throughout Carol's illness. It was the last thing I wanted to be doing but that was our reality for the time being.

In Florida, being lesbian was not something you could talk about openly. It was not something you read about in the papers. It was not something you encountered in the community—or if we *did* encounter other lesbian and gay people, they kept quiet about it. Only when LGBTQ+ issues became a legislative issue at the state or national level did it make its way into the news.

Carol and I knew that there was a place we could be living where there was a thriving gay community: Greenwich Village, New York. We never talked about moving there for two reasons. First, we couldn't afford to live there. And secondly—and most important—was the fact that Carol had to live in a warm climate due to her Raynaud's Syndrome.

We planned a vacation to San Francisco with Tommy and John and stayed at a Sheraton Hotel. We were at a winery right outside the city, having a great time, when suddenly Carol started getting stomach cramps. All she was doing at the time was sipping wine. Before I knew it, she was laying on a bench in violent pain, unable to get up.

I lay her head in my lap so she wouldn't feel the hardness of the bench, and held her hand.

Tommy and John were concerned, saying, "We really should take her to the hospital!"

"We have to go to the hospital," I said to Carol.

"No, I don't want to! Can we wait?"

"We have to go now," I said.

We took Carol to a hospital emergency room in San Francisco and explained to the medical personnel that she had scleroderma. When the admitting nurse saw Carol doubled over in pain, she took her into an exam room right away.

The nurse checked Carol's vitals and said that her blood pressure was very high. This was no doubt from the stress caused by the pain. Then they took Carol for some sort of test on her stomach. The results revealed a stomach ischemia—sort of like a heart attach of the stomach muscle. Of course, this was due to the scleroderma.

The doctor explained, "Ischemia of the stomach is a condition in which the blood and oxygen don't reach the stomach…"

"Do you think the wine tasting could have triggered it?" Carol asked.

"No," said the doctor. "If anything, the wine would have been good for you. But we are going to need to admit you."

Seventeen

It was scary to think that we were admitting Carol to a hospital we knew nothing about, and where she had no relationship with any of the doctors. They would keep her in the hospital for as long as it took to stabilize her—but they could only treat her symptoms.

Carol's internist, who was still her primary scleroderma physician at this point, had warned us that this sort of thing was bound to happen. It was just a matter of what was going to happen and when.

By continuing to live her life, Carol was taking the risk that anything could happen at any time. But what else could she do? Her only other option was to lock herself indoors and never leave the house, out of fear that something would happen when we were in an unfamiliar location.

Tommy, John and I returned to the hotel to sleep. When I called the hospital during the night to check on Carol, I was told that she was resting comfortably but was no better. That's how low the bar was set— they were aiming to simply keep Carol comfortable. It was the best that any of the doctors could do for her, given that systemic scleroderma is incurable.

I knocked on the door of Tommy and John's room to let them know about the update I had gotten on Carol. I told them what was going on, but they didn't say anything. They didn't seem to know what to say or how to handle the situation.

The following morning, they came to me and said, "We've booked a flight. We're going home."

I couldn't believe my ears. They knew that I needed their support. I was upset that they were leaving me to deal with Carol's hospitalization alone. I didn't understand how our best friends could do such a thing to me, and I felt betrayed. Since they didn't give me a reason for leaving so abruptly, I was left to figure it out on my own.

They're fleeing because they can't deal with it! I said to myself.

Neither of them had ever witnessed what scleroderma does to a person before. So, they were undoubtedly stunned, scared and in shock. They had no idea how to handle the situation. Even to this date, they have never offered any explanation. I have never demanded one either.

Carol and I spent about a week in San Francisco, with her remaining hospitalized the entire time. I would sleep at the hotel, get up and have breakfast at the hotel restaurant. Then, I would walk the short distance to the hospital and sit with Carol in her hospital room during the day. Thankfully, the hotel gave me a reduced rate when I explained the reason I needed an extended stay.

During the last years of Carol's life, we would spend plenty of time in hospitals, just as we did that week. I became accustomed to sitting in her hospital room with her while she slept or rested. There were only two times during Carol's protracted illness that she had an episode while we were out of town. This trip to San Francisco was one of them.

By the time Carol was released from the hospital, she was stable enough to fly home. We did stay one extra night at the hotel before flying home, just to give her a chance to recuperate from being hospitalized.

Sadly, being released from the hospital was not an indicator that Carol was now healed. There was no getting well. Scleroderma would continue to ravage her body. Of course, we kept our hopes up nonetheless.

I knew that hope and a little bit of magical thinking was the tonic that kept Carol going. That's what made it possible for her to deal with her gruesome situation. So, I joined her in that hope for a miracle or a cure, even though in my heart of hearts, I was resigned to the reality.

On the flight home, Carol was chilled, so I got a blanket and covered her up. We talked about what had happened. We also talked about whether we would continue to travel, knowing that she could have another episode at any time. We agreed that we wanted to continue to travel for as long as Carol was able. Walking was already hard for her, due to the worsening condition of her feet. We were all too aware that the clock was ticking.

We did not hear from Tommy and John when we returned home. I couldn't believe that they didn't call to check and see how Carol was doing. I couldn't bring myself to pick up the phone and call them. I still felt so hurt and betrayed over them abandoning us in San Francisco.

It was clear that they had no idea whatsoever how to handle the situation. They were our best friends—and we were theirs. I'm sure it was painful for them to accept that Carol had a terminal illness.

I was hurt, but I understood how they felt. We had all being going along, living our peaceful lives. The shock of Carol's diagnosis came out of nowhere.

Meanwhile, Carol and Arline's parents, Sarah and Max, mentioned to them that they were planning to renew their vows sometime soon. They didn't have a plan yet, so Carol and Arline decided to surprise them with a party. They invited their parents to a party and told them that it was being held for friends of theirs.

Arline was living in Florida by that time. So were Sarah and Max, who had followed Carol and me to Florida and lived about two miles from us. They had swept under the carpet the fact that Carol and I were in a romantic relationship. On a surface level anyway, they acted like they were fine with Carol and me being a couple.

Sarah and Max thought the party was being held in honor of someone else. On the day of the party, we drove them to the event site.

When we arrived at Kelly Green's, a country club in Fort Myers, Sarah and Max were a bit surprised to see all of their relatives there, along with my parents. (Carol's parents and mine had become friends over the years.)

There were other guests there, as well, that they wouldn't have expected to see at a party for the friends who were supposedly the guests of honor. When they saw the rabbi I had asked to officiate, they might have been tipped off. He was from Temple Beth-El where I worked at my first job in Fort Myers.

"What's everybody doing here?" they asked Carol and me.

"It's your party! It's the party you would have made for yourselves for the renewing of your vows. We did it for you."

Sarah and Max were so happy, they started crying tears of joy. They were about to have the party they could never have had if they had to pay for it themselves.

We had a chuppah (a canopy beneath which Jewish marriages are performed) at the bema (the altar). Sarah and Max walked down a little aisle under an archway created by canes held by groomsmen standing across from each other. Among the groomsmen were my father and the father of Carol's cousin, Shelly.

(Shelly happened to be a lesbian who was in a relationship with a woman named Barbara. Shelly was also an LGBTQ+ activist. Carol had never wanted to be bothered with Shelly when she was younger. She feared that her association with Shelly might somehow result in her being outed. Carol's father and Shelly's mother were cousins.)

I was so happy for Sarah and Max—and yet I couldn't help but feel a little resentful. I thought to myself, *They get to have two weddings and I don't even get to have one!*

I was able to hide these feelings of resentment for Carol's sake. I knew how important this day was to her and her parents. For that reason, it was also important to me.

While I was walking around the party, mingling, Shelly's parents approached me and started a conversation. I had met them at Carol's parents' place and seen them there over the years. I sat down and talked to them.

"Arlene, I want you to meet my Shelly and my Barbara sometime," said Shelly's mother.

When Carol had initially told me that her cousin Shelly was a lesbian, and her parents were coming to the party, I said, "You have a cousin who's a lesbian? Really? Why aren't you in touch with her? Let's call her!"

"I can't! I have to be out if I call her."

I went around the party, looking for Carol. When I found her, I told her that I'd met Shelly's parents.

I said, "They want us to get together with them! We should do it. It's time to meet other people. And we have something in common with them! They've been together a long time, just like us."

I was surprised and excited when Carol agreed. We had just a few gay and lesbian friends. And, Carol's insistence that we remain in the closet cost us straight friends. She worried that people might figure out that we were together and out her. If she had already been out, it wouldn't have mattered.

That was sad to me—but nothing was sadder than the fact that Carol's denial of who she was led to her getting scleroderma. I was sure of it. Her body became sick from suppressing the truth for so long.

After the party, I said to Carol, "Call Shelly!"

This was one of those times when Carol listened to me and did as I asked. I think she understood how important it was to me to have friends, even if she thought she could get by without them. And now that we were out of touch with Tommy and John, we didn't really have any other close gay or lesbian friends.

Carol called Shelly, sending her into a state of shock. She couldn't believe that, after so many years of keeping her distance, Carol was actually willing to open the door to her.

I got on the phone and arranged a get-together with them. Shelly and Barbara decided to come visit us in Florida, and stay at a nearby vacation destination called Sanibel Island.

They came and spent a night at our house before heading to Sanibel Island. We went out to dinner at The University Grill, a lovely restaurant, and had a great time. We totally hit it off with them. It was so good to meet another lesbian couple, especially people that Carol already knew.

By this time, Carol and I had moved from the initial house in Fort Myers and were living in a house we'd had built for us. It was located in a planned community called Parker Lakes. We had a two-bedroom place, and used the second bedroom as a guest room.

"Why did you wait so long?" I said to Carol after Shelly and Barbara had left for Sanibel Island. "We could have been friends with them all these years!"

Shelly and Barbara would end up moving to Fort Myers. They told us that they had such a good time while they were here, and enjoyed our visit so much, they wanted to live nearby. It wouldn't happen right away, but when it did, it brought us so much joy.

Eighteen

Carol was experiencing a lot of pain in her big toe. It turned out that there was an infection in the bone of the toe.

"This is a result of the Raynaud's," explained the doctor. "The fact that your toes are turning blue tells us that the circulation is blocked, and blood flow is not reaching the big toe."

The doctor told us that there was only one possible treatment that might save Carol's toe: putting her in a hyperbaric chamber. This was intended to oxygenate her entire body. Unfortunately, the treatment failed to stop the infection in Carol's toe.

The doctor explained that sometimes a thumb can be used to replace the toe as a prosthetic. Then he said that in Carol's case, the lack of oxygen getting to the toe would eliminate this as an option.

"I am so sorry to tell you this," said the doctor, "but we're going to have to amputate the toe." (It was the big toe on Carol's right foot.)

Carol was already hurting in both feet. The pads given to her by the doctor to provide cushioning were not helping. So, it was painful for Carol to walk, even before her toe was amputated.

The doctor promised Carol that he would try to do the surgery in such a way that she could still wear regular shoes. He would do his best with the surgery to preserve her gait. But, without a big toe, your balance is thrown off.

Finding out that Carol was going to lose her big toe was devastating news for us both. We went home and cried. This was a terrible thing to happen to a shoe lover like Carol.

"It's only a toe," said Carol through her sniffles. That was my Carol, always looking on the bright side and clinging to hope.

"I know," I said, "but it's *your* toe!"

"Well, it could have been the whole foot," she said. "At least it wasn't the foot. We have to look at things positively. Do you think we'll still be able to go to Sedona with Shelly and Barbara?"

"Of course, we can go! If you can walk, we can go!"

We scheduled the surgery for the spring of 2004, at Health Park Hospital in Fort Myers. The surgeon told us to expect the surgery to take about three hours. On the day of Carol's surgery, I waited for what seemed like an eternity. The doctor finally came out. He wanted to talk to me before I saw Carol in recovery.

"Well, it was a success," said the surgeon. "And Carol should be fine. I got out all the bone that was infected…"

The only issue the doctor anticipated in terms of Carol's recovery was the lack of oxygen and blood getting to the foot.

The surgeon told me that I could go into the recovery room to see Carol. When I saw her, she was awake and seemed to be doing well. She was even hopeful that everything would be fine. Unfortunately, her pain was intense. There are so many nerve endings in our feet, and the surgeon had to cut through bone. The pain pills seemed to do the trick, thank goodness, during the couple of days that Carol spent in the hospital.

When Carol was released from the hospital, she had to teach herself how to walk on that foot all over again. The fact that her gait returned to normal was a testament to just how adaptable we are as people.

We had our vacation planned for the summer of that same year. Carol was getting steadily better, and by the time of our vacation, she was well enough to go. She was on permanent disability by this time, so she didn't have to worry about getting time off work.

Even though I agreed that we should go ahead and go on vacation with Shelly and Barbara if Carol was up to it, I had my concerns.

Not long after her diagnosis, Carol had a heart attack, and had to see a cardiologist. She was only forty-five years old at the time. It is possible that she could have had a heart attack even if she hadn't had scleroderma; there's no way to say whether the illness played a part. Then she had to see a vascular doctor for problems with her veins.

On the day of Carol's heart attack, we were at home in Fort Myers. "I'm not feeling well," said Carol.

"What's the matter?"

"I feel like I have the flu. I'm really lightheaded and everything's hurting...my arm, my jaw."

Instead of calling an ambulance, I said, "Let's go to the hospital."

When we got there, the doctor took her vitals and said, "You're having a heart attack!"

Carol and I gave each other a look that said, "What? Are you kidding me?"

The doctor gave Carol a shot of TPA (tissue plasminogen activator) to clear whatever was blocking her heart, and she started to feel better. Thankfully, an echocardiogram and other tests they did on Carol at the hospital showed no damage to the heart caused by the heart attack. Considering the other medical issues Carol was dealing with, we were grateful for this small blessing.

Our vacation trip with Shelly and Barbara was going to include stops in Sedona and Las Vegas. We all bought cowboy hats and were really excited to go. Carol and I flew to Vegas and Shelly and Barbara met us there. The four of us stayed at the Luxor Hotel. By sharing one room with two beds, we were able to stay in a more luxurious hotel. The fact that the four of us were able to share one room was a testament to how well we all got along.

While we were in Las Vegas, we saw a couple of shows, including the Blue Man Group. We had a good time and I appreciated the group's funny antics, but their blue faces scared me. We also played blackjack and the nickel slots. We didn't want to lose too much money, but it was hard to tear ourselves away from the casino.

We were there for three days and had a great time. Thankfully, none of the hotel staff questioned why four women were sharing a room. Little did they know that one of us was a lesbian activist.

Since Shelly was a leader in the lesbian community, she was able to fill us in on everything she'd been involved in throughout the years. She told us about the women's marches and other happenings in the women's movement. It was amazing to see photos of her and other women marching, wearing equality buttons.

It really touched me to hear stories of the lesbian community fighting for equal rights. At that time, very little progress had been made. I couldn't in a million years have imagined that my relationship with Carol would one day lead *me* to become an instrument of change in the LGBTQ+ movement.

When we were ready to leave Vegas and head to Sedona, we rented a car. Shelly, Barbara, and Carol split the driving duties between the three of them. Surprisingly, Carol's recent toe surgery didn't impact her ability to drive. I left the driving up to them. I was a new driver and didn't yet have the confidence to drive on the narrow roads between Vegas and Sedona.

It was a great drive and we passed the time playing car games. When we reached the Grand Canyon, we stopped to sightsee. I stood at the edge of the canyon and looked down. It was so deep, I could barely see the bottom. I thought to myself, *If someone fell down there, you'd never find them!*

I had never in my life seen anything approaching the Grand Canyon, with its immensity and grandeur. (A later trip to Alaska would have the same kind of majesty and scope.)

Despite Carol's serious health issues, she held up like a champ. She was always strong, and never showed any pain or stress related to her illness. It was only when she went into a full-blown Scleroderma medical crisis that you would even know there was anything wrong with her. And yet she lived with mounting medical problems, starting with her stomach, then going to her toe. As each new Scleroderma issue arose, Carol had to see another specialist.

We arrived in Sedona in the early evening, just in time to see the sun setting over the beautiful red rocks. Instead of arranging hotel accommodations, we had rented a condo. Once we got ourselves settled, we went to a nice restaurant and had a steak dinner. Then we returned to the condo for a good night's sleep. We had exhausted ourselves with the drive from Las Vegas.

The next morning over breakfast, the four of us talked about what we might want to do that day. Carol said that she'd like to go hot-air ballooning. I am scared to death of heights, but my desire to be with Carol was stronger than my fear. I didn't know how many more adventures Carol and I would have together. I didn't want to miss even one chance to be together. I went out of my way to do the things she wanted to do.

Barbara also had a fear of heights, and no compelling reason to overcome it. So, she stayed behind while Shelly, Carol and I went in search of a hot-air balloon company.

When faced with the actual balloon, I had to take a deep breath and calm myself. I climbed up the stepstool and got inside. The balloon held eight, so along with us three girls, there were five other people. I decided that my best bet for surviving my fear of heights was to stand in the middle. Carol meanwhile was holding onto the edge.

At one point, I got up my nerve and moved to the edge. I was thankful that the balloon never went up that high. Before I knew it, we were safely touching down in a little brook. Our toes got wet through the bottom of the balloon. Then, the operator got the balloon airborne again, and we sailed over the red rocks and the mountains. It was exhilarating to see such majesty from above. Best of all, none of us experienced any air sickness.

On the downside, the balloon did sway from side to side. It was unnerving to see the fire keeping the balloon afloat. I would not repeat the experience, but I'm so glad I overcame my fear in order to experience it with Carol.

We spent about five days in Sedona. We toured a beautiful church and went on a mountain excursion where we saw mountain goats. I loved the southwestern architecture of the homes, and the beauty of the rocks.

On our trip, we were walking a lot. So, it was no surprise that Carol's right foot started to hurt. Carol traced the pain to a stitch her doctor had sewn into the incision site as he wrapped up the surgery. Carol's foot had been slow to heal due to lack of blood and oxygen. Any time she touched the area of the toe where the stitch was, it hurt.

Barbara came to the rescue. Although she was in the banking industry, she was a nurse at heart. So, she went right into nursing mode, got a pair of tweezers, and removed the stitch for Carol.

With the stitch out of her toe, Carol felt better and was able to walk much more comfortably. So, we were able to enjoy the rest of our time in Sedona. I was so happy that, despite her health problems, Carol and I had gone ahead and taken this vacation with Barbara and Shelly. I'm glad we didn't let our concerns over potential medical disasters keep us from going.

That trip was in the summer of 2004. Later in 2006, Barbara and Shelly sold their house and moved down to Florida to be near us. Once Carol had overcome her fear of being outed by befriending her cousin

Shelly, the four of us bonded rapidly. After enjoying many happy visits with us, Barbara and Shelly had fallen in love with Florida.

They were tired of the snowy winters in upstate New York and ready for a change. And Shelly had dialed down her activism in the New York lesbian community, so it was unnecessary for her to continue living in New York. After many years of being a high-profile lesbian activist, and fighting the good fight, she had become exhausted. It was hard to keep fighting for the cause when she wasn't seeing many meaningful changes in the women's movement.

Shelly didn't work, so she could live any place she wished. And Barbara was on the verge of retiring. This meant that they were both free to live wherever they chose.

Carol and I were so excited that Shelly and Barbara had made the decision to leave New York and move to Fort Myers. We had all gotten very close, as evidenced by our ability to spend extended time together in a hotel room.

Nineteen

By this time, Tommy and John had faded from our lives somewhat. After they left the hotel on our San Francisco trip, they drifted away from us. We didn't hear from them nearly as often after we moved from New York to Florida. They were a little bit upset that we had moved to Florida. And, I was more than a little upset that they had left me alone in San Francisco during Carol's hospitalization.

It was sad to see how much we had drifted apart, considering how close we had all been when we lived in the same building. During the summertime, Carol and I made a trip to New York to visit Tommy and John. When we went to see them, we had to pay for our tickets. John, on the other hand, worked for Delta, yet he and Tommy only visited us a total of three times in all the years we lived here. We had a spare room, so they wouldn't have even had to pay for lodging.

I was often tempted to talk things through with Tommy and John. Carol felt it would be better to leave things alone. I did say to John one day, "I don't understand why we rarely talk and you never come down to Florida to see us!"

He glossed over the question, saying something like, "Everybody's busy these days."

It hurt me to know that John wasn't willing to talk things through with me. That was our only hope of ever being truly close again. But I accepted the situation and didn't push him further.

Shelly and Barbara set out to find a home as close to us as possible. They looked at virtual drawings of one place they liked, only a mile from where Carol and I lived. Carol and I went and looked at it for them and told them all about it. This enabled them to buy it, sight unseen, without having to make a trip down to see it.

Their new home was in a brand-new development under construction. It was a coach home—a two-level villa where one tenant lives on the top floor and a separate tenant lives on the bottom.

We were all thrilled to be living near each other at last. No more plane flights just to have a visit. Now all that was standing between us and a visit with them was a short car ride. It was heavenly.

In the springtime, Shelly and Barbara came to Florida in advance of the moving truck carrying their belongings from New York to Florida. They stayed at a rental apartment while their house was being built and put their belongings into a storage unit. When their house was completed, Carol and I helped Shelly and Barbara unpack, set up their house and settle in.

From then on, we were constantly back and forth between our house and theirs, like Lucy and Ethel on the iconic T.V. show, *I Love Lucy.*

The four of us got along so well, and there was so much harmony between us, we naturally wanted to do everything together. When we went on vacations together, the four of us could share one room with two beds. Typically, four women in one bathroom would be difficult, but not with us. We functioned so well as a foursome, it was easy to find workarounds for any challenges we faced.

Some lesbians prefer to hang out only with other women. Not Carol and me. We also enjoyed the company of gay men. It wasn't unusual for us to go to gay-and-lesbian house parties. At one of these parties, we met a group of women, and hit it off with them. They invited the four of us to join them on a women's cruise to the west coast of the Caribbean. Altogether, there would be six couples in our group.

The cruise was operated by Olivia Cruises, a cruise line owned by two lesbians and openly advertised as such. Living in our town of Fort Myers, Florida put us in the ideal spot to take a cruise. So many cruises left from either Miami or Fort Lauderdale. So, we didn't have to pay for flights to the location where the ship would be boarding.

This was the first cruise the four of us would be taking together, and we were very excited. Shelly, Barbara, Carol and I drove in one car, and the other four couples were going to meet us at the dock.

We parked in the lot across from the ship dock, and brought our luggage to the check-in area. We got two adjoining rooms with balconies furnished with tables and chairs, so we could take full advantage of the view.

That night, we set sail. We spent the evening dancing to oldies music. It was a real treat to get to slow-dance with Carol. Unless we were at a gay-and-lesbian event, we couldn't usually dance together because it wasn't considered "normal." People would stare and wonder what was going on. So, we usually sat out the slow dances.

Not only were we allowed to dance together aboard the ship, this lesbian cruise line celebrated the couples. They even had a cake the size of a tabletop for any couples onboard who happened to be celebrating an anniversary.

In the days when I dated men, danced with them, and made out with them, I enjoyed the closeness. But I didn't know what intimacy was really supposed to feel like until I fell in love with Carol. It was a major milestone in our lives, to be on this lesbian cruise, free to dance all night and hold each other close.

We felt so free. In that environment, women dancing together and holding each other close was considered normal. As we danced, I thought back to the night so many years before when Carol and I visited that women's club. I could still see us sitting there, frozen to our seats in disbelief.

The following day, the four of us spent time lounging by the pool or in the casino. (Gambling was legal at sea.) And the day after that, disaster struck. It happened right after we had our photos taken by the ship photographer. He was snapping away, and before he finished, he had taken fifty photos.

Out of that batch, there was one photo that perfectly captured the love that Carol and I shared. In the photo, Carol was seated and I was standing above her, with my arms wrapped lovingly around her. We both look dreamy and caught up in the rapture of love.

After the photo session, the four of us headed downstairs to dinner. We had to walk down two flights of carpeted stairs to get to the dining room. I was worried that Carol would have trouble walking. She was in pain but by holding onto the railing, she made it down the stairs just fine.

I began to descend the stairs in flat sandals. I was almost to the last step when my eyes played tricks on me. The stairs and the landing blurred together, as they were the exact same color. Because I couldn't see where the step ended and the landing began, I missed the last step.

I collapsed onto the floor in excruciating pain. Carol, Shelly, and Barbara rushed to my side, along with the other couples who were with us on the ship.

They called for help and soon ship personnel arrived with a wheelchair for me. They took me to the first-aid office. My leg was x-rayed, and the x-ray revealed a broken tibia—the bone that runs from the ankle to the knee. The ship nurse wrapped up my leg in an Ace bandage and gave me some pain pills. Then she gave me the option to be flown back home for medical care. (They may not have had a doctor on the ship; or if they did, he may not have been the kind that sets bones.)

I declined to be flown home. It was only the second day of the cruise when my injury occurred. I didn't want to miss the rest of the cruise. I knew that Carol's diagnosis was a death sentence and I valued every moment we spent together.

I would be stuck in a wheelchair for the duration of the cruise. I had to have someone push my wheelchair to every outing, and I had to use the elevator when we went to meals. As I rolled along the hallways, I would look up at the guests we passed. I tried to make eye contact and smile but very few people acknowledged me.

I learned from this experience just how uncomfortable it makes people to deal with someone with any sort of impairment. Perhaps it reminds them of their own vulnerability. I too was uncomfortable. Being so vulnerable and dependent on others was unusual for me. I am usually the caretaker of others. It was strange to be the one in need of caretaking. The experience of being briefly wheelchair bound gave me greater compassion for those with physical challenges.

In the evenings, Barbara would wheel me down to the casino. I would have normally enjoyed a little bit of gambling, knowing I had a set limit on how much I was willing to lose. But the fact that everyone around us was ignoring me in my wheelchair spoiled the experience for me. Feeling invisible really bothered me.

Though we were all made somewhat miserable by my injury, we did our best to enjoy the remainder of the cruise. When it came to an end, things got complicated. Rolling me off the ship wasn't really an option because there were steps. So, instead, two guys who worked on the ship carried me off in my wheelchair.

Carol took me to see an orthopedist as soon as we got home. I had worried that by staying on the cruise and waiting to see the doctor until we got off the ship, I'd suffer repercussions. But the doctor told me that the bone was healing well, and I had nothing to worry about. I did not require surgery to reset the bone—but I did have to wear an orthopedic boot for eight weeks to stabilize the bone while it healed.

Carol was out of work on permanent disability, so we had plenty of time together while I was laid up. And, thankfully, since neither Shelly nor Barbara were working, I had plenty of looking after while I healed. As for me, I took about a week of medical leave from Lynx Services, where I worked as a facilities manager. (By the time I retired in 2012, I would have been working there for a total of fourteen years.) When I was ready to return to work, I went into the office with the boot on my leg.

Twenty

By this time, Sarah and Max had been living with us for a year or so. In 2005, Carol had come to me and said, "My parents are getting older and they're afraid to live alone."

Sarah and Max were afraid that one of them would fall ill and have no one there to look after them. They were also concerned about finances. The small amount of money they earned from their Social Security and pension checks was insufficient for them to pay for their own place.

"What do you think about them moving in with us?" Carol continued.

I knew in my heart that it would be disastrous to have Carol's parents living with us. But I told Carol that I thought it would be fine. I knew that it was important to her to be able to look after her parents in this way. I couldn't say no to her. I knew that putting her parents in a home or in assisted living was not an option for Carol.

"…But this house is too small for the four of us," I continued. "It will never work in this house. We'll need to buy a bigger house."

"Well, we could sell this house and buy one of those courtyard homes with the mother-in-law house." We ended up buying a house at the height of the market and overpaid for it.

Courtyard homes are set up in such a way that you walk in the front door of the main house and find yourself in an open-air courtyard. It has a patio, a pool, and a separate entrance leading to a mother-in-law suite. It was like having a pool house, only it was connected overhead to the main house. When you passed the door to the mother-in-law suite and kept going, you came to the door leading into the main part of the house. Then all four of us shared the kitchen.

Unfortunately, Carol's parents used the great room in the main house as their living room. This was a terrible arrangement for all concerned. None of us had any privacy. If they had been able to spend time in their own private living room, the situation would have been more tolerable for all of us. As it was, it was extremely stressful. Since scleroderma was affected by stress, this was a recipe for disaster.

As you entered the main house, there were three bedrooms and a bath. One of the bedrooms served as an office for Carol's father, one was a den/office for Carol and me, and the third was the bedroom I shared with Carol.

Both Carol and I felt her parents' disapproval of our relationship. It totally altered our lifestyle. (Much later in life, Carol's assistant from work would share with me that Carol always felt like she'd made a mistake by moving her parents in with us. She recognized the terrible effect it had on our relationship.)

We wouldn't hold hands in front of Carol's parents, even though we were in our own home. And I wouldn't cook for us in our kitchen because it was important for Carol's old-world Jewish mother to take over the kitchen and make it her domain. So, despite the fact that I happen to be a gourmet cook, I was edged out of my own kitchen. We sometimes ate dinner with them, but when we had a craving for something in particular, we ate out.

The kitchen situation caused endless arguments between Carol and me. I would explain to her that it was just easier for us to eat out. I knew that it was important to her mother to have dominion over the kitchen. I didn't want to end up in a power struggle with her over it.

The situation was made even more horrible by the fact that Carol's parents did not drive. They couldn't go anywhere unless Carol took them. They were dependent by nature and not the type to call a cab and go somewhere on their own. It was like having houseguests that never left. They left us in complete charge of their comfort and their happiness.

Rather than learning to accept that their daughter and I were a couple, Carol's parents completely ignored the fact. They saw us sharing a bedroom, but they averted their eyes rather than trying to come to grips with it.

Sarah and Max had been living with us for about six years by the time that Carol and I started thinking and talking about marriage. Barbara and Shelly started talking about it first. Same-sex marriage was illegal in the state of Florida at that time. I had both gay and lesbian friends who had wanted to get married and investigated possible solutions. They discovered that same-sex marriage was legal in New York.

Up until then, Carol and I had felt that having an actual marriage certificate would be nice but was unnecessary. We knew that our love was strong and our relationship solid, and that was good enough for us. But now, Carol was getting sicker and sicker, and was on permanent disability. She did know she would die of scleroderma, but she didn't know how or when the disease would claim her life. Any of her organs could have hardened at any time, causing her death.

One day, Carol said to me, "You know, we should really get married. If we don't and something happens to me, you won't be able to have my benefits."

"But the way things stand with same-sex marriage laws," I said, "I won't be able to anyway!"

"But if we get married now, and the laws change later in Florida like they have in other states, you'd be eligible to collect my benefits. I think we should do it."

This was one of the only times in our many years together that Carol took the lead in our relationship. She really pushed for us to get married. She knew that it would make my life easier after she was gone if I had a marriage certificate.

One day while playing canasta with Shelly and Barbara, one of us four said, "Why don't we just go to Iowa and get married? We've never been there."

Somehow, Iowa didn't feel quite right. New York seemed like the right choice. Three of the four of us were New Yorkers—and Barbara was originally from Boston but had spent a long time in New York.

It was decided. We would fly up to New York in October of 2011 and get married. We knew that we were playing beat the clock. If we didn't get to New York and get married quickly, we'd be out of luck. By November, temperatures in New York would be too cold for Carol to tolerate.

We had been through enough New York winters to know how hard they were on Carol's body. Neither one of us would forget her sitting in a hot bathtub in our apartment years earlier, as we tried to get her toes, black from frostbite, to thaw out. We had a short window of time to plan everything and that window would soon close.

On the trip, there would be Carol and me, Shelly and Barbara, and Laura and Leenie—good friends of ours that we'd met at one of the parties we attended when Shelly and Barbara moved to Florida. They often went to ballgames with Carol and me. They had gotten married a few years earlier in California. They were coming along for support.

Carol and I, and Shelly and Barbara would be staying in New York at the condo Tommy and John had bought in Beechhurst. The guys would be accompanying us to city hall, as well. Laura and Leenie would be flying up separately and staying at a place in Manhattan.

I wasn't worried about tension between Carol and me and Tommy and John. Those issues only rose up between us when they were in New York and we were in Florida. When we were all in the same town, and in the same room, we had a wonderful time together and were as close as ever.

If I had held against Tommy and John the fact that they shut down when Carol got sick and didn't come to Florida to see us, that could have been the end of our friendship. But I kept a special place in my heart for them. So, we all remained on good terms.

I was not going to get my dream wedding, where I had a big wedding gown and all my friends and family were in attendance. This wedding was being driven by necessity and the feeling that we needed to get officially married before Carol was too ill to go through with it.

We talked about planning some kind of reception in Florida to take place after the marriage ceremony, but it never came to pass. Sadly, Carol's declining health made it impossible.

As for wedding attire, we all agreed that there was no need to get dressed up for a wedding ceremony taking place at city hall. We decided that we would wear street clothes. Shelly and Carol decided that they didn't want to wear veils during the ceremony, but Barbara and I wanted to wear them. So, we planned to go shopping and find matching veils with headpieces.

Thankfully, on the day of our flight to New York, Carol was feeling fine—or if she wasn't, she never let on. The flight was incident free. When we got off the plane, we were picked up by Tommy and John. Our faces lit up at the sight of each other. After not seeing each other for a year or two, we were all excited and happy to be together again. We exchanged hugs and kisses all around. We all loved each other very much and our reunion was really heartwarming.

As we got into the car, we all talked excitedly about getting married. We talked about how, over the years, we had been forced to accept the fact that marriage was not in the cards for any of us. And yet, here we were, about to get married in front of our closest and dearest friends.

Hawaii had been the first state to reverse their laws on same-sex marriage. Then a couple of other states followed suit. By 2011 when Carol and I got married, it had only been a few years since the tides began to turn and the states gradually started to change their laws.

Tommy and John had decided that they didn't need to get married. "We're just going to do a domestic partnership ceremony at city hall," they explained.

"If you're going to do a ceremony at city hall anyway," I said, "why not go ahead and get married?"

"It's not the right time for us, financially speaking," they explained.

I didn't entirely understand but I dropped the subject. I knew they had their reasons and I wanted to be respectful of their privacy. What was clear was how happy they were for Carol and me. They were thrilled for us—and thrilled to be there to witness the occasion.

For a while, during the time when we were all living in the same building in New York, all we had was each other. Both of us couples had been living in the shadows, keeping our relationships secret, terrified of what might happen if the truth got out.

After we had chatted for a while, I told Tommy and John that we needed to buy flowers for all four of us, and veils for Barbara and me. So, Tommy, Barbara and I went shopping. The first stop we made was at a Michael's Art Supplies store to look for veils.

They had exactly what Barbara and I were looking for. So, we each bought one and then headed to the florist. We bought bouquets of red roses bound with wire, so we could each hold one during the ceremonies. My red-rose bouquet sits to this day, dried, in a vase in my home.

That night, we all played canasta at Tommy and John's, hung out, and talked about the upcoming weddings. We also got caught up on each other's lives. When it was time to get some sleep, Tommy and John slept in their room, Barbara and Shelly slept in the spare room, and Carol and I slept on a blow-up bed in the living room.

The next morning when we woke up, Carol and I were so excited. We couldn't stop talking about the fact that we were actually getting married, after believing for so long that this day would never come. The date was October 21st. Laura and Leenie had also gotten married on October 21st, a few years earlier in California. We didn't plan to get married on the same date but that's the way it worked out.

We knew that, although we were legally allowed to get married in New York, Florida would not recognize our marriage—for the time being, anyway. We would be prevented from filing joint tax returns and enjoying the myriad of benefits that come with having your marriage officially recognized as legal.

I was also privately troubled by the fact that I would not be listed as Carol's next of kin on her death certificate when she passed. I knew that bringing up the subject would upset Carol, so I kept that particular concern to myself. But it bothered me terribly. I knew that hospitals were very bureaucratic in nature.

It would have been so much simpler if Florida had recognized our marriage. Another alternative would have been for Carol and me to move back to New York, where we had lived happily for so many years before she got really sick. But living back in New York was absolutely out of the question now. Carol's body simply could not handle the cold weather anymore.

Despite the fact that our marriage would not be recognized by the State of Florida, it was still terribly important to both of us to get married. Our reasons were twofold. First and foremost, we wanted to get married because we loved each other. Secondly, we knew that, little by little, state by state, the nation was changing its policy. So, we realized that there might very well come a day when our New York marriage would be recognized in every state in the union, including Florida.

Barbara and Shelly were equally excited over their wedding day. Tommy and John cooked a wonderful bacon-and-egg breakfast for all of us. Meanwhile, we were waiting for Laura and Leenie's arrival. When they got to the condo, we all took some photos with Barbara and me wearing our veils. Then it was time to head to city hall.

Twenty-One

All eight of us weren't going to fit in one car. So, we split up into both Tommy's car and John's, for the drive to Kew Gardens City Hall in Queens.

There was a long line of people outside, all waiting to get married. The day was cold for October, and we were all worried about Carol. But there was nothing we could do about it then. We had come all that way. We weren't about to turn around and board a plane home to Florida. So, we had Carol go stand close to the building where it was warmer.

Carol was wearing hand warmers and insulated socks. Sadly, that didn't keep her feet from hurting. None of the rest of us felt the cold the way Carol did, but we felt her distress and that was upsetting to us. We huddled up and did our best to stay warm, while we willed the line to move faster.

We were waiting in line with gay and straight people of all races and colors. Most of the couples were straight but, being in a big city like New York, no one gave us any sideways glances. That's one of the great things about big cities. They tend to be very progressive and inclusive.

We were all chatting and making small talk as we inched our way closer to the moment that would change our lives forever. There was a palpable excitement and energy buzzing through the line, connecting all of us. After waiting in line for what seemed like five hours but was probably more like forty-five minutes, we finally reached the entrance to the courthouse and went inside.

When we got inside the clerk's office, I was looking around, thinking to myself, *This is so cold looking! It's not at all the way I pictured my wedding!* Then I reminded myself, *Well, we are finally getting married. That's the important thing.*

We were taken into a drab room to fill out our paperwork and pay the fee for the marriage license. Then we were ushered into a room with a vine of fake flowers decorating the ceiling. *Okay,* I said to myself, *this feels a little better, a little less sterile.*

When we met the clerk who would be marrying us, I felt even better. She was a lovely, heavyset black woman with a warm, beautiful smile. And she was genuinely excited to be marrying us. We decided that Shelly and Barbara would go first. As the clerk led them through the traditional vows, Laura and Leenie, Tommy and John, and Carol and I were all openly crying.

Shelly and Barbara's ceremony lasted no more than five minutes. Then it was our turn. Our ceremony flew by as well. After Carol and I said our vows, the clerk declared, "I now pronounce you spouse and spouse. You may kiss each other!"

I cried through the entire ceremony, thinking of what a miracle it was that we were getting married after so many years. Getting married is something that all people who are in love should be able to do—and it was happening at last.

We left city hall around noon and headed into Manhattan for lunch. We ate at an Italian restaurant recommended by Tommy and John. We were over the moon as we enjoyed our celebratory lunch. In lieu of a wedding cake, we ordered a special chocolate dessert.

We all raised our glasses and made a champagne toast to long, happy, healthy marriages for all of us. Of course, not so far in the back of my mind was the fact that Carol was sick and would never get well.

There was no sign that the restaurant knew what we were celebrating that day. We all figured that was just as well. We felt it was wise to keep things quiet and discreet. After lunch, we went back to Tommy and John's house and sat around talking about how life had been during all those years when we had been forbidden to marry. We could hardly believe it had finally happened.

We were all physically and emotionally spent, so we turned in early that night. As for Laura and Leenie, they caught a train downtown to their hotel and then headed home. In the morning, the first thought on my mind as I opened my eyes was that I was now a married woman.

I thought back to all the years Carol and I had waited to reveal the truth about our relationship. And I thought back on all the years we lamented the fact that we were unable to get married. It had been such a long journey and we had arrived at the altar at last. It was hard to even fathom that it was real. I felt like we were living in a dream.

We stayed for another couple of days at Tommy and John's before heading home to Florida. We went to the site of the World Trade Center to see how the construction efforts to rebuild were coming along. It was still not quite finished.

Standing there, looking at it and absorbing the meaning behind the monument, I was filled with emotion. Carol and I may have lived in Florida, but we were New Yorkers at our core. Scanning the wall with the names of all the fallen brought tears to my eyes.

We played canasta every night, just as we had done all those years earlier when we lived one floor apart. Canasta was one of our favorite pastimes, and we were happy to be able to play cards with Tommy and John again. We taught Shelly and Barbara the game, and they were able to join in.

Then it was time for me and Carol, and Shelly and Barbara to return home to Florida. Carol was a real trooper on the trip. Her excitement over getting married overrode whatever pain she was experiencing. It kept her going. She was always so brave, soldiering on despite how she felt.

She managed the plane flight home without incident. As always, she kept quiet about any pain or discomfort she may have been feeling. I always marveled over her courage. When we got back to Florida, we sat Carol's parents down.

Carol said, "Mom and Dad, I know we told you we were going to New York on vacation. Actually, we went there to get married."

They looked at us with a surprised look on their faces, like they had no idea we were a couple. And yet, Carol had told them the truth many years earlier. And, they lived under the same roof with us!

"You can do that?" they asked. "You can get married?"

We explained that same-sex marriage was legal in New York but not in Florida, and that was why we had gone there to get married.

They looked at us blankly. I'm sure this news about us getting married made our relationship more real. Carol and I were now a married couple—and that was a reality they could not handle.

They listened to our news and then swept everything back under the rug, as usual. They had been that way their entire lives. They lived into their nineties and never changed.

Twenty-Two

There were many same-sex relationships that survived for twenty, thirty, forty years until same-sex marriage finally became legal. During those decades when Carol and I weren't married, we could have walked away from each other at any time. This only goes to show that it is the love and commitment that is the glue holding two people together—not a marriage certificate. Nevertheless, knowing we were legally married was the most wonderful feeling.

For a brief moment in time, we were over the moon. It was as if we had stepped out of all the struggles we had lived with for so long and entered a world without pain or worry. The excitement and relief of getting married carried us along like a pink cloud.

Then, once we returned home, we were quickly brought down to earth. There on the calendar was a list of doctor's appointments. By this point, Carol was seeing doctors several times each week.

The list of her ailments was growing by the week. Now, Carol often woke up with terrible stomach cramps; the blood flow in her right leg was obstructed; and she was experiencing muscle wasting. She had appointments with a stomach doctor, a heart doctor, and a vein doctor. After a while, it began to seem like we were living at doctors' offices. And it wasn't like these doctor's appointments were going to change the course of the future.

I began to find it surreal the way the doctors treated Carol. Instead of treating her systemically, they treated only the symptoms in specific regions of her body. If she was having trouble with the veins in her leg, she went to a vein doctor. Stomach trouble? Off to see a gastroenterologist. Foot problems? We made an appointment with the podiatrist.

I was frustrated by the doctors' failure to see Carol as a whole person and her symptoms as part of a larger picture. Maybe knowing that there was no real cure caused them to take this treat-the-symptoms-only approach. In any event, I found it disturbing. Carol was literally falling apart right before my eyes. Yet, there was nothing anyone could do about it.

I often pondered the fact that her sister had lupus, another autoimmune disease. It made me wonder about the family's genetic predisposition to autoimmune diseases. I also know that keeping all your emotions inside creates all sorts of physical problems. So, I often thought about Carol's family's habit of swallowing all their emotions. I was sure that this contributed to their tendency to get autoimmune diseases.

I know how much stress it caused Carol to keep her feelings and our relationship hidden throughout our lives. I always felt badly knowing that our love—something we both cherished so much!—was such a cause of distress for her.

Carol wanted to live so badly, she couldn't bear to talk about dying. That was one of the reasons she kept quiet about it. I'm sure she was also trying to protect me, just like I was trying to protect her by honoring her wish to refrain from talking about her illness.

It would have been great if she had been open to talking about the fact that her scleroderma was eventually going to kill her. Instead, we each dealt with our feelings and our fears privately. It was such a lonely way to handle it.

The next three years flew by in a blur of doctors' appointments. Thankfully, Carol had medical benefits from three different sources, so her care was paid for in its entirety. We were very fortunate in that way.

During those three years, we tried to schedule two trips—one to the Panama Canal and one to Alaska. We were both indulging in a bit of wishful thinking in planning these trips. When the time for the Panama Canal trip was almost upon us, we realized that it was completely unrealistic to think we could go. Carol was having major stomach and intestinal problems, which affected her on a daily basis.

"I don't think we should go on this trip," I said, hating to be the one to bring it up. "I really think we should cancel. We'll be stressing out the whole time, worrying that something could happen while we're far from your doctors. It's just not worth it."

The unspoken truth behind us having to cancel our trip to the Panama Canal was this: our traveling days were behind us.

I often asked myself whether Carol was even aware that she was going to die of scleroderma. An online forum I found on her computer after her death provided the answer. She had been privately going into this online scleroderma forum and sharing fears and feelings she didn't share with me.

Many times, I said to myself, *If it were me and I had this illness with its fatal prognosis, I think I would end it all.*

As Carol got sicker and sicker, I continued to wonder how on earth she managed to keep going. Sometimes she was so sick and in so much pain, she had to sleep in a chaise in the living room. She was more comfortable in that chaise than she was in bed.

I felt so helpless being unable to take away my wife's illness and suffering. Toward the end of her life, I entered therapy. By that point in time, I was in need of some support, myself. I needed to talk to someone about the fact that Carol was dying—and I couldn't talk to her about it directly.

In the Jewish culture in which I was raised, it is unusual to see a therapist. But I knew that if I didn't talk to someone about how I was feeling, I could end up sick, myself. When I worked for the community center in New York, I was surrounded by social workers. Being around them on a daily basis convinced me of the wisdom of seeking help when you need it.

I was also able to talk to Barbara confidentially about my feelings about Carol's illness. Carol was very dear to Barbara and Shelly, so they understood how I was feeling. We would sit together and cry. Shelly, Barbara and I all agreed that we needed to do whatever we had to do for Carol. And what she needed was for us to keep from mentioning the fact that she was going to die.

The next chapter of Carol's illness was really horrible. She was no longer getting blood or oxygen to her right foot, thanks to a vein issue. (When Carol lost her toe, it was from this same foot.) She was told that her foot would have to be removed up to the ankle.

The doctor assured her that she could get fitted for a prosthetic after surgery. This was a world-renowned doctor and we both trusted him completely. So, Carol and I went online to look at prosthetics. I knew in my heart that she would not have much time to walk on the prosthetic foot. The removal of her foot was the death knell, the beginning of the end.

"We'll just remove it and I'll get a prosthetic," said Carol. "Everything will be okay."

Each time we got to the next terrible milestone in her declining health, Carol adjusted to it. It was amazing to behold. At every turn, she put aside the knowledge that she was going to die and forged ahead, wearing rose-colored glasses.

I knew the cost to Carol of losing her foot. She didn't mention her heartbreak over losing her foot, so neither did I. Throughout our lives together, I always put Carol first. I was the stronger of the two of us, thanks to the fact that I came from a more functional family. Carol didn't deal with things head-on like I did, so life was easier for me.

Carol told her parents about her upcoming surgery. Her parents had been watching her go downhill, right along with me.

She and her mother cried together. Her mother said, "Why you and not me? I'd rather this be happening to me! I've already lived my life."

Despite their dysfunctional family dynamic, Carol was still very attached to her parents, and especially her mother. Meanwhile, they were still living in our home with us. This was an extra burden I could have done without, especially during the period leading up to Carol's death. But, what could I do? I concentrated all my attention on Carol.

Meanwhile, Carol's sister, Arline, stepped up her efforts to be there for their parents. She came over more often and took Sarah and Max to the store and to run other errands.

I told Tommy and John about Carol's upcoming surgery. "You may want to come down for this surgery," I said. "It's really major and I'm not sure what's going to happen. I would appreciate having you here for support."

They said they would try—but they never made it. They never offered any explanation, either. They simply excused themselves. I knew how upset they were over Carol's worsening condition, and I knew that the surgery was probably more than they could handle.

I said to myself, *She's losing her foot. What is she going to lose next? And how long before I lose her entirely?*

I was very frightened but I tried not to let on. It was the unspoken agreement between Carol and me that I would always be the maternal one, looking out for her and protecting her. In this case, she wanted me to protect her even from the truth. But it was a truth that could not be ignored. I knew that she knew the truth in her heart of hearts, despite her resistance to talking about it.

After the surgery, the doctor came out and told me that he had removed Carol's foot. "We'll see if it's enough," he said. "I'm not sure."

When I asked him to clarify, he said that he wasn't sure whether the surgery had done the trick in terms of stopping Carol's pain. Throughout an excruciating and relentless night, it became clear that they needed to go back in. This time, they removed Carol's leg below the knee.

I was living in an ongoing nightmare, sleep-deprived and terrified. I was up most of the night with Carol, forgoing sleep while she dozed off and on. Thankfully, Shelly and Barbara came and sat with me. They were a real blessing from God.

I thought back to when I first met Shelly and Barbara, and I remembered how Carol had steered clear of Shelly for all those years. She didn't want to be associated with Shelly and her overt efforts on behalf of the LGBTQ+ community. Now, the four of us were as close as we could be. I don't know what we would have done without them during Carol's illness and beyond.

Carol's double surgery was followed by a period in rehab. About two days into Carol's stay in rehab, she started to feel really ill. It was clear that something was dreadfully wrong. So, she was transported back to the hospital by ambulance. I said to myself, *This isn't good. I have a bad feeling about this.*

Carol's blood pressure was spiking, so her cardiologist came to see her at the hospital. He administered some tests on her heart.

"I just want to go home," said Carol. "Can I do that? I want to lie down in my own bed and see my dog."

The doctor agreed to let Carol come home.

I realized Carol probably had a feeling that the end was nearing. The doctor probably knew that the end was near as well. Barbara, Shelly and I got Carol into a wheelchair and drove her home. After the five-minute drive home, we managed to get Carol's wheelchair inside the house, where her parents were waiting.

Twenty-Three

I sent Barbara and Shelly home, telling them that they should go get some rest. I said that I could take it from there. I wanted some alone time with Carol.

It was afternoon by this time. "I need to run to the store and pick up a few things," I told Carol.

"Okay," she said, "but don't take too long."

I was only gone for fifteen or twenty minutes. When I got back home, Carol was distraught. She told me that she was feeling profoundly unwell. "Something's not right," she told me.

I quickly called Shelly and Barbara to ask them to bring over their blood-pressure monitor. (Ours wasn't working.) When I checked Carol's blood pressure, it was dangerously low. I called the doctor, who told me to get Carol back to the hospital as quickly as possible. I had a feeling that the doctor sensed what was coming.

"I'm not going," said Carol. "I want to stay here."

My higher self had taken over by this point and I sensed the nearness of the end. I could not bear to have Carol die in the house. "Carol, you have to go! I'm calling an ambulance." Then I thought better of it and decided to just have Shelly drive us there, since she and Barbara were already at our house.

We went back and forth for a few minutes, with me insisting that Carol go, and her refusing. Finally, she agreed to go. So, Shelly drove us all to the hospital.

An emergency-room nurse took Carol's vitals. Then she sent her out into the waiting room while they prepared a room for her. I was sitting with Shelly and Barbara when Carol joined us. Suddenly, she pulled her hood over her head.

"What's the matter?" I said. "Why are you doing that?"

"I'm cold. I want to cover my head…" Then she was very still and quiet.

After passing a hideous night of being hooked up to machines, Carol began to slip away. I had to make the hardest decision I had ever made in my life. I told them to disconnect her from the ventilator that was breathing for her. (I was the one with Carol's power of attorney for medical matters.) I knew this was Carol's wish because she had been gesturing to me to pull the plug.

Hospice was now present in the hospital room, administering a strong narcotic to help ease Carol into her last moments. I covered her with a blanket and held her hand.

"I love you so much," I said softly. "And I'm so sorry for what you're going through. It's okay to let go, honey. You'll be at peace now."

After what seemed like forever, I felt Carol's hand go limp in mine. She was gone. The love of my life passed away at 4:15 in the afternoon on March 13th of 2014.

I was so glad I had trusted my instincts and insisted that Carol be in the hospital for her last moments. It was devastating enough to let go of her in the hospital. I could not even imagine how it would have felt to have to say goodbye to her in our home.

Arline had been at the hospital with us, but she left to pick up her parents and bring them back. Sarah and Max had been with us at the hospital, but they were hysterical. That was making Carol even more anxious, so I had sent them home. I knew that Arline would soon be returning with them.

Given that Sarah and Max had spent decades pretending that Carol and I were even not romantically involved, much less married, I was not optimistic about how they might behave when they got back. I couldn't envision a scenario where they would suddenly graciously start recognizing me for what I truly was: Carol's bereaved wife. I sensed that I might be facing a fight from them.

When Arline, Sarah and Max returned to the hospital about an hour after Carol had died, my concerns were validated. It quickly became obvious that Carol's parents were trying to take the upper hand and control the arrangements. Sadly, a power struggle ensued between them and me.

They said that Carol should have a Jewish burial.

I said that, no, Carol had been very clear about her wishes. She had specifically stated that it was her wish to be cremated. And I told them that her paperwork confirmed this.

They said that, being Carol's parents, they were the most important relationship in Carol's life. Therefore, they should be the ones to handle her end-of-life arrangements.

I was sensitive to the fact that Sarah and Max were Carol's parents and were understandably bereft. There are few things in life more heartbreaking and unnatural than having your child die before you. And, as I said, despite their family dysfunction, Carol was very close to them.

I tried to be respectful of the fact that they had just lost a child. But, when all was said and done, I was Carol's spouse. I said that as her wife, I was the most important relationship in her life. She was married to me!

Ultimately, I decided that there was no point in arguing with Sarah and Max. I walked away, knowing that Arline would drive them home. I didn't need their permission to follow Carol's healthcare directive.

Her wishes were very clear. She wanted to be cremated. And, as her healthcare surrogate, I planned to do exactly that.

Barbara and Shelly helped walk me through the next steps, including funeral arrangements.They opened their home to me, and I accepted. I left the dogs in the care of Carol's parents.

Strangely enough, on the day after Carol's death, I saw an article in the newspaper about the ACLU. According to the article, the ACLU had filed a class-action suit on behalf of eight same-sex couples who were married outside Florida. Just like Carol and me, these couples' marital rights were being denied by the State of Florida.

I said to myself, *I have a feeling something's going to happen and I'm going to need some help. Maybe the ACLU could add me into this class action lawsuit!*

I didn't know what kind of trouble I was likely to encounter, but I had a gut feeling that it was coming. It was like the sixth sense that some people seem to have about the weather—the feeling that tells them when a storm is gathering in the distance and is headed their way. I had the sense that I was about to face some serious backlash and needed to prepare myself.

I figured that the Social Security office was likely to refuse to give me Carol's benefits. That was certain to be an issue. I didn't have the mental wherewithal at the time to envision what other challenges I might be about to face related to whether or not my marriage to Carol was valid and legal. But I knew that more challenges were coming.

I decided that it was time to call in the cavalry. So, I took out my phone and called the ACLU that very afternoon. I told them my story. I explained that Carol and I had been married in 2011 in New York. And, I explained that Carol and I had been living in Florida where same-sex marriage was not recognized. I also explained that Carol had died in Florida.

During the call with the ACLU, they instructed me to write a paragraph documenting what I had just told them and email it to them. After I spoke with the ACLU, I went back to my house. I wanted to check on the dogs. I also needed to pack a bag so I could continue staying with Shelly and Barbara.

When I got home, Sarah said to me, "It would have been better if you were a man."

I felt like I had been punched in the gut. "What do you mean?"

"It just would have been better if you were a man and this wasn't like this," said Sarah.

And then, for the first time ever, I told her, "Carol was my wife! Whether you two like it or not."

They had never accepted this fact, but in that moment, I threw it right in Sarah's face.

"Look," I explained, "I'm mourning my wife! And now I'm getting grief from you? I don't care what you think. She was my wife, and that's all there is to it."

"But we're her parents!"

"I understand that," I said, "but I'm her wife! I'm the person who makes decisions about Carol, not you."

Even as I was saying these words, I knew that I didn't have much of a legal leg to stand on. All I had in my favor was a piece of paper—Carol's medical directive. I had also been assigned in her Will as executrix of her estate. And I was Carol's healthcare surrogate as well as being the holder of her power of attorney.

I am sorry to say that a terrible, screaming argument followed. Carol's parents were screaming at me, and I was screaming right back. All those decades earlier when Carol and I were young, we had tiptoed around. We always tried not to offend anyone with the truth about our relationship. And ever since, her parents had been swallowing their feelings and disapproval as best they could.

Now, everything that had been buried blew sky high. We were emotional, raw, devastated, and drained. They were brokenhearted over the loss of their daughter, and without the capacity to relinquish the reins to me as her wife. And I was mourning my wife, and without the self-control to avoid an argument.

Carol had always been the peacemaker between her parents and me, the mediator. We had always understood that her parents were unhappy over us living together as a couple. Despite the fact that Sarah's own brother was gay, Sarah and Max simply could not accept the fact that their daughter was a lesbian—a married lesbian.

I told Sarah and Max that, without Carol's benefits, I would no longer be able to afford to keep the house. And I explained that they needed to have Arline find them another place to live.

I knew that I would never receive Carol's pension. She had been given the option to name me as a beneficiary when she began receiving her pension benefits, or to take the higher amount. Afraid to admit to my existence, she had chosen to take the higher amount.

As you know by now, she was always deathly afraid that someone at her work would find out that she was part of a lesbian couple. Taking the higher amount saw us through her protracted illness—but we could have lived on the lesser amount.

Twenty-Four

After Carol died, I knew I could not afford the mortgage alone, so I stopped making the payments. This caused my credit score to take a real dive. My credit was already suffering because all of our credit cards had been in Carol's name. So, the credit-card companies believed it had been years since I'd had a credit card. This meant that I couldn't even get a credit card of my own, which I could have desperately used during that period of time.

Carol did have an insurance policy with a death benefit. Thank G-d for that. I took $10,000 of the money and gave it to her parents so they could apply it toward a new place to live. They had their sights set on the entire proceeds from Carol's insurance policy. They were also hoping to keep everything in our house.

While all of this was unfolding in the aftermath of Carol's death, I stayed at Barbara and Shelly's house. I felt comfortable, safe and protected there. I will be eternally grateful for their love and support during that difficult time. They were angels in my life.

I will spare you all the ups and downs of trying to divvy up Carol's belongings. Suffice it to say that her parents and I did not see eye to eye on this process. It was not done in a loving spirit on either side.

On their end, they were horrified by my continued insistence that I was Carol's wife and entitled to the rights that went along with that title. And on my end, I was mortified by their refusal to recognize that truth. None of us conducted ourselves with the grace and generosity that would have been ideal. It was such a difficult time, all the way around.

I briefly tried to return home—but so much confrontation and chaos ensued between Sarah and Max and me, I realized it was not worth it to be there. I threw my hands up in the air and returned to Shelly and Barbara's house.

When I got to the funeral home to make the arrangements for Carol, I had Barbara and Shelly with me. Sarah, Max and Arline met us there. We all had to sit in a room together and do what needed to be done. We were barely speaking to each other.

I picked out an urn for Carol's ashes, and small urns for her parents and Arline. Each urn would contain a little bit of Carol's ashes. Meanwhile, Carol's parents reiterated their wish that Carol be buried rather than cremated. They knew by then that it was a lost cause. I had my wife's medical directive in writing and that's all there was to it.

The funeral director came into the room, carrying Carol's death certificate. This was the first time I had laid eyes on it. As he showed it to me, he said, "I just want you to know that I know that you and Carol were married. But the State of Florida does not recognize your marriage as legal. So, it is going to say on the Death Certificate that Carol was single...never married."

His words were like a stab to my heart. I was in shock. I had not known whether a death certificate was governed by state or federal law. Had it been governed by federal law, our marriage would have been considered legal, and my wife's marital status would have been listed as "married."

I figured that being left off Carol's death certificate was bound to make it impossible for me to collect her Social Security benefits. Now I knew why I'd had such a strong gut feeling that I needed to call the ACLU.

I had known I would have some issues when Carol died—but I didn't know what they might be. Having never gone through that experience before, I had no clue as to what I would be up against. I suspected that having a marriage that was legal in New York but not recognized by Florida would cause some sort of problem. I had no idea that it would result in me being left off the death certificate entirely.

The funeral director continued, saying, "Carol's father or mother will have to sign the death certificate."

They signed the certificate, thereby allowing me to proceed with the cremation. They may not have even realized the impact of signing the document. They were too stressed and devastated to be able to think straight. Had they been in a different state of mind, they may have realized that this was their opportunity to prevent me from going forward with the cremation.

Shelly, Barbara and I began to plan a celebration of life ceremony for Carol. We decided that we would like to do something at the Unitarian Church. I first became acquainted with the Unitarian Church when the Southwest Gay and Lesbian Chorus to which I belonged sang there. After we sang that day, I stayed for the service and loved it. They are very warm and welcoming toward the LGBTQ+ community.

I jumped right in and got involved with the church, joining the welcoming committee there. Then I introduced Barbara, who was a non-observant Catholic at the time, to the church. Carol had no interest in attending services at any church, but she came with me once in a while. Shelly is a secular Jew. So, Barbara started coming to services with me. Like me, she appreciated the liberal attitudes of the church. We both needed that.

The three of us put our heads together and tried to scare up the money for the celebration of life. I wasn't sure where I was going to get the money. I was sixty-six at the time and had been collecting my Social Security benefits since I was sixty-two. So, my checks were not large.

I'd had no choice but to take Social Security early so I could help look after Carol during her illness. With just my Social Security check to live on, I was in bad shape financially. And, I was not receiving a pension.

Carol and I did have a tiny savings account. I knew I would need that money, but I decided to use it for the celebration of life. I figured I could replace the money when the proceeds of Carol's insurance policy were disbursed.

I decided I wanted the celebration of life gathering to be large. Since Carol and I had such a small marriage ceremony at City Hall, we had missed out on getting to have a real celebration.

When I told Carol's parents that I was planning a celebration of life at the Unitarian Church, Max told me that he was planning a service at the synagogue.

"I'll go with you to the synagogue," I said, "and you can decide what you want to do once we get there." So, we made an appointment with the rabbi.

I went to the synagogue with Max, Sarah, and Arline. When the rabbi asked Max what sort of service he would like to do for Carol, he couldn't make up his mind.

"Well," said the rabbi, "we could have a very small service, family only. We could do it right now if you like."

We agreed and the service was held right then and there. Sarah, Max, Arline and I were the only ones in attendance. The rabbi said a little blessing and conducted a traditional Jewish service. Then the rabbi talked to Max about sitting shiva at our house for four days. I had no objection. I felt that it was the right thing to do.

We sent out notices, letting everyone know we were having shiva for Carol. We sat shiva, mostly in the evenings. Arline, Sarah and Max were there, along with friends of mine who stopped by to pay their respects. Things between Carol's family and I were as civilized and peaceful as they could be, given the tension between us.

I went back to Shelly and Barbara's house and we began to plan the celebration of life ceremony. I called the Unitarian Church and spoke to the reverend about officiating at the service.

(I also made arrangements with the reverend to place in the church's memorial garden a bench and table in Carol's memory. The plaque on the bench bears this inscription: *With love to Carol from Arlene.* Once in a while, I go to the garden, sit on the bench, and remember. I also had a little urn of Carol's ashes spread there.)

The service was gorgeous. I arranged for delicious hot hors d'oeuvres and desserts from Renee's, one of the finest caterers in town.

Carol's ashes were delivered in a beautiful urn with dolphins on it, which sat in an urn holder that looked like a throne. The Gay and Lesbian Chorus sang at the ceremony. I did not join them for that performance. I sat with Barbara, Shelly, and Carol's family.

Tommy and John came down for the funeral and flew back that same night. I could see how deeply they were mourning Carol. Yet, I couldn't help but feeling a little angry with them. They had visited so rarely while Carol was sick. Ultimately, my love for them won out and I forgave them.

I couldn't believe how many people kept piling into the church. There were about two hundred people in attendance. So many of them were people Carol knew from work. As I gave my speech about the two of us and our love, I knew it would be a shock and a revelation to some of Carol's coworkers.

I talked about how Carol and I had known and loved each other all our lives. I talked about our life together and how hard we had fought for our relationship.

One year after Carol died, on April 20th, 2015, I attended a reception in Washington, D.C. with nearly eighty same-sex marriage plaintiffs from around the country. Some of them, like me, had lost their spouses. All of us had filed lawsuits with various state entities (in my case, the Florida ACLU) to have our marriages recognized in the states in which we resided. We had all won our lawsuits and our marriages were recognized in our specific states. At that time, however, there were still certain states in which same-sex marriage remained illegal.

(In January of 2014, my attorney, Daniel Tilley, had called to tell me the good news. We had won the lawsuit, and the judge issued this decree:

Decree

There is no good reason to further deny Ms. Goldberg the simple human dignity of being listed on her spouse's death certificate. Indeed, the state's refusal to let that happen is a poignant illustration of the controversy that brings us here. ~ The Honorable U.S. District Court Judge, Robert L. Hinkle, August 21, 2014

I also received an updated death certificate for Carol. Under "Marital Status," it had originally stated "never married." Now it was amended to state: "Married to Arlene Goldberg." I was so happy, I had started to cry.)

The event in D.C. took place at 6:00 in the evening. Earlier that same day, the Supreme Court oral arguments were held related to overturning the remaining state bans on same-sex marriage. On June 26th of that same year, the U.S. Supreme Court decided in our favor and the bans were overturned. Same-sex marriage became legal in *all* states. I feel so proud to be a part of the group of people whose stories have shown America that it's time for the freedom to marry.

Then, in mid-August of 2015, I was honored to speak at the Gil Foundation's semi-annual conference for donors in Dallas, where they raised $2.9 million dollars for the LGBTQ+ community in the South. At the event, I told my story. I also had the pleasure of introducing Mary

Benauto and Robbie Kaplan, the remarkable, out, strong attorneys who had represented before the U.S. Supreme Court the plaintiffs from those states where same-sex marriage had still been illegal.

The following is the speech I gave that day:

"In 1960, Carol Goldwasser and I were just two little thirteen-year-old girls in the Bronx when fate introduced us. Who would have thought, back then, that we were meant to spend forty-seven years together?

We lived and loved in New York until Carol could no longer take the cold because of her illness. We didn't know it at the time, but Carol had a rare autoimmune disease called scleroderma. So, we moved south to Fort Myers [Florida] where we lived for the remainder of our days together. For most of that time, we lived in the closet. So, I felt like this. This is a poem I wrote called Together Forever:

They don't care if we're not free,

Together alone we will be,

Not free to show the way we feel,

It just is not a really fair deal,

In love forever, hiding away,

Sharing our feelings, day after day,

I love you, my darling,

Together we're free,

Who cares what they're thinking?

We'll always be.

And in October 2011, thanks to the work of so many of you here tonight, we were legally married in New York State... Then, on March 13, 2014, at 4:15pm, Carol left this world to finally get a well-deserved rest and be rid of the pain that had haunted her consistently for a very long time. I understood and I didn't blame her.

When you lose someone you loved for more than forty years—you can never prepare for that. And instead of being able to mourn, I faced countless challenges navigating Carol's death. I wasn't allowed to make decisions for her. Her father had to sign for her cremation. If he hadn't been available, they would have searched for another next of kin—and it wouldn't have been me—in accordance with Florida law.

Instead of being considered Carol's wife or next of kin, I was listed as her "informant." Her death certificate listed her as single—despite our more than four decades together.

So, it felt like fate when I learned that the ACLU of Florida had filed a lawsuit on the exact same day Carol passed. I recognized the sign, contacted them and they agreed to amend their existing lawsuit to include my case. Here we are fourteen months later, and thanks to the ACLU, our attorney Daniel Tilley and Judge Hinkle, Carol's death certificate has been amended.

It now lists Carol as married to me at the time of her death. It also lists the "informant" (me) as her wife. Florida didn't treat us as married in life, but at least the state saw us as married in death. Wow, that was big! It was the first time a same-sex couple married outside of Florida was recognized on a Florida legal document.

This journey has been bittersweet for me, but I also believe our battle must continue. We still have much more to do until equal rights are totally realized for our community. Carol's death propelled me into action. I did not stop with winning marriage equality in Florida on January 6th, 2015.

I know firsthand that marriage means a lot, but it isn't enough. There's a lot more to do to ensure full equality for LGBTQ+ people. I'm continuing to fight on all fronts to ensure that the LGBTQ+ community is equal under the law. Transgender issues, bullying in the schools, employment equality. Our work isn't done until we are all equal.

Southwest Florida is a very conservative area and ours is a community that has long lived in the shadows, until now. We have stepped out of our closet and will continue to march towards full equality. It is truly inspiring to be in this room surrounded by so many people who have been committed to full equality for LGBTQ+ Americans.

I'd like to give a great big thank you to all associated with the ACLU, from the bottom of my heart, for your hard work to ensure freedom and equality for everyone throughout this United States."

Afterword

In December of 2014 (the same year Carol died), I had received the Voice for Equality Award from *Equality Florida*. We had about two hundred and fifty people at their Annual Inaugural Black and White Ball. I wore a black gown to this formal affair—the very first LGBTQ+ event ever held in Lee County.

The mayor of Cape Coral attended, but there were other dignitaries we had invited who did not choose to grace us with their presence. Among those who did not accept us and chose not to attend were the mayor of Fort Myers and the county commissioners.

Any time they see me coming, they run. I am always going to them with issues. I have been on a mission to change things here. In fact, that's why I am still living in Fort Myers—to make a difference! In the time I have been here, fighting the good fight, I have made many great friends. I also stay because of them.

Things only began to change in this area in 2011 when I opened my community center, *Visuality*. We have programs for LGBTQ+ youth between the ages of thirteen and twenty-five, as well as adults of all ages. We also have support groups.

After Carol passed, I also founded an LGBTQ+ Chamber of Commerce, which continues to grow in membership numbers. I am the go-to person for newspapers, radio and other media. They call on me all the time related to LGBTQ+ issues.

I even had business cards made up for myself that say *Arlene Goldberg, Southwest Florida LGBTQ+ Activist.*

I'm involved in activism because I was repressed and in the closet for twenty years. I know what people face as an LGBTQ+ person. I help people find places to live. I sit on panels in business and organizations, helping them learn to be sensitive to the LGBTQ+ community.

The activism work I do can be draining and exhausting. It's easy to get discouraged and burnt out, knowing that change happens at a snail's pace. You work and work and feel like you're getting nowhere. And yet, little by little, change does occur.

I try to encourage others to come out of the closet. I tell them, "Staying in the closet doesn't help you—or anybody! All it does is keep you in the closet. And when you're in the closet, people don't even know you're there. It's almost like you're invisible. You are who you are. Coming out and learning to be yourself frees you."

From My High School Yearbook
(1965 Graduation)

My inscription to Carol:

Dear Carol,

Even though we aren't as close as we used to be, there will always be that warm feeling between us. I know you are the sincerest person I have ever known. I know that someday soon, we will again be close friends.

Love always, your friend, Arlene.

Hers to Me:

Dear Arlene,

Well, we went through a lot together. And, we both have to face the fact that we'll have a lot more to go through. I only hope the problems ahead will be very insignificant. Still I know that in the future, we'll both still be the best of friends as always. We'll conquer any and all problems the way we did before—*together!!!*

Love always, Carol

Acknowledgments

Reverend Allison Farnum…Thank you for your love and support, and for praying with us in the hospital. It meant so much that you were there.

Aunt Rhoda Cohen…Thank you for your ongoing support and love.

Barbara Kuzniar and Shelly Goldstein…Thank you, with much love, for standing by Carol during her last few weeks. And for sheltering me so I could breathe again after her death. I am so grateful for the years the four of us had together as travel buddies and very best friends. I am looking forward to many more.

Daniel Tilley…Thank you for being the best attorney anyone could have, and for becoming a special friend to me.

Howard Simon…Thank you for leading the charge, with the ACLU of Florida, for marriage equality. You have become a dear friend.

John Chaputian & Tommy Locicero…Thank you for being there as Carol and I commenced to spread our wings. And, thank you for all the gourmet dinners, canasta games on warm wonderful evenings, and shared vacations to such special destinations.

U.S. District Judge Robert Hinkle…Thank you for your caring and sensitive decision to direct the attorney general to modify Carol's death certificate. Your directive made my marriage to Carol the very first same-sex marriage recognized in the state of Florida. None of us in the LGBTQ+ community will forget the dream you made come true for so many by making same-sex marriage legal in the state of Florida.

Les & Phyllis…Thank you for accepting me for who I am, and for making coming out to both of you so easy and comfortable.

Heidi…Thank you for the closeness we shared.

Mom and Dad…Thank you for your love and honesty while bestowing upon me an upbringing that made it possible for me to blossom into who I am today. I am who am because of you. I will always keep your love deep within my heart.

Nurse Susan Adkins…Thank you for watching over Carol while she was in the hospital so many times. It made us both feel secure.

Peg Walsh…Thank you for helping me through the grieving process and moving me into the light.

Susan Christiano…Thank you for being there for me, standing by me during and after my grieving process, and encouraging me to start a new life. I love you, my friend.

Toto and Lacey (my fur babies)…Thank you for being there for me during many a dark day, and brightening them with your puppy kisses.

Trish Better Black…Thank you for taking on the very first ever LGBTQ+ bereavement support group in Lee County.

Developmental Editor, Vivien Cooper…Thank you for helping me resolve Carol's death by reliving my life. And for "getting me" and becoming a good friend. You do what you do fabulously, and I'm thrilled you did it for me!

And, last but not least, thanks to everyone who showed up for Carol's celebration of life. It meant the world to me.

A Special Author's Note
To You In the LGBTQ+ Community
Who Find Yourselves in The Closet or in Distress

Before I close, I want to say a few words to any of you still living in the closet, or in distress, depressed or suicidal over your sexual orientation or gender identification. Please reach out and ask for help and support! There are so many resources available to you, starting with the National Suicide Prevention Lifeline, which can be reached at 1-800-273-8255. A simple Google search will turn up many more resources.

I also want you to know that I empathize. I have been there myself. When I was around fifty years old, I thought about killing myself. I had lost my job because my position had been eliminated.

Here's what happened. I was working for the government in Lee County, Florida. During the annual salary review, the company checked with other municipalities to see what they were paying employees in comparable positions. Then, they would adjust our salaries accordingly.

That year, mine was the only salary not reviewed. The construction services manager, Hans, who was my boss's boss, arbitrarily decided not to.

Hans was a big, strapping man with a heavy German accent. And I felt that he was anti-Semitic. He never treated me the way he treated everyone else. In those days, Jews were a rarity in Lee County, and I was the only Jewish person in the entire office.

When Hans refused to do my salary review, I went over his head. I went to our human resources department and said, "I need a review on my salary, and Hans didn't do mine."

Hans got wind of what I had done and came to me, angry. "Why did you go to H.R. behind my back?"

"Because you didn't do a salary review on my position! That's unfair."

"I didn't want to," he said.

"Well, I'm the only one whose salary you didn't review. So, it sounds to me like something else is wrong. Do you have a problem with me?"

"No, I'm just not going to do the review." He wouldn't admit to having any bias toward me. And he didn't seem to feel the need to explain himself, either.

We were at a standoff. I wasn't going to just swallow his explanation—and he couldn't fire me because I had excellent reviews.

So, he found a sneaky way to get rid of me. It took him several days to devise a way to do it without it coming back to haunt him. When he finally landed on the perfect solution, it was airtight.

One week after that confrontation with Hans, my boss, Robert, told me that my position had been eliminated. He told me that I had only one more week of work and then I'd be gone.

I started to cry. I knew that Hans was behind it but what could I say? I couldn't very well tell Robert, "I know that Hans was behind you eliminating my position."

I had no way to prove that. Hans had never said or done anything overtly anti-Semitic. I could feel his aversion to me, but I had no proof of it.

I remembered back to an incident from my childhood. When I was a kid, living in the projects, I was involved in musicals and other activities at the neighborhood YMCA community center. One summer, a group of kids from the Midwest came to the Y for a summer visit. Somehow these kids realized that I was Jewish.

"Where are your horns?" one of them asked me.

"What do you mean, 'where are my horns?'"

"Jews have horns on their heads!" the kid said.

"Well, *this* Jew does not have horns on her head!"

"But my mom told me that *all* Jews have horns on their heads."

There was another instance later in my life where I heard that repeated again.

Anyway, when they eliminated my position, they gave my tasks to my secretary—the one I had trained so well.

Carol was also working for Lee County, but in a different office. On the day my position was eliminated, I came home crying hysterically.

"Hans let me go!" I told Carol. "And they want me to work one more week. I don't even know how I can go back there after this! I'm heartbroken."

Carol did her best to comfort me, saying, "Don't worry, Arlene, you'll find another job!"

I was inconsolable. I found the injustice of it so hard to swallow. I had been let go without cause, even though I had proven myself to be a good worker.

I had spent so much of my life controlling outcomes. I carefully lied to my parents about Carol for years, even though I hated doing so. I took charge of situations with Carol when I felt that what I was doing was in our mutual best interest. In every way, I had felt completely in control of my life.

This was the first time I had ever been blindsided. My life had taken a direction that was completely beyond my control and I had no idea how to handle it.

I did not see Hans once during my final week at work. It was obvious that he was going out of his way to avoid me. My friends at work had two going-away parties for me. Everyone was sad to see me go. I was the saddest one of all. I shed a lot of tears that week.

I continued to suffer over losing my job. I didn't know how to process it. I would be at home thinking about being let go from my job. It made me feel so sad and unmoored. I was sitting there all day doing nothing. It was a quick jump from that line of thinking to a feeling that I was not only doing nothing all day, but I was *being* nothing. Losing my job made me feel worthless and useless.

My brain chemistry was suddenly off. One day, I was driving along the street and I thought to myself, *I should turn the steering wheel and crash my car into that wall!*

My brain had a mind of its own, so to speak. I couldn't seem to control what I was thinking. I felt like I was possessed. In that moment, I didn't care how my suicide death would have affected Carol, my parents, my former coworkers, or other friends and loved ones. When you're in that state, you're not thinking about anyone else.

Carol was working at the time that I had that momentary impulse to crash my car into a wall. Thankfully, I was rational enough to think to myself, *Oh, my goodness! What am I thinking?*

I drove myself straight to my doctor's office for some anti-depressant medication. I hadn't even learned to drive until right before Carol and I left New York. Imagine if one of my first driving outings had led to me using the car to kill myself!

About the Author

Arlene Goldberg is a recognized and beloved leader and pioneer in the LGBTQ+ community, and the recipient of the 2014 Voice for Equality Award given by Equality Florida. She was one of the plaintiffs in the groundbreaking ACLU class-action lawsuit related to same-sex marriage laws in Florida. Thanks to the outcome of that lawsuit, Arlene and her wife, Carol, made history in 2014 by becoming the first same-sex couple to have their New York marriage officially and legally recognized by the State of Florida. (Sadly, Carol did not live to witness this great victory.)

Arlene cofounded *Visuality* in 2011, thereby establishing the presence of the LGBTQ+ community in Lee County—a region in southwest Florida previously devoid of such resources. She created and participates in panels through *Visuality* that are designed to educate and sensitize the southwest Florida community to the needs of its LGBTQ+ population.

In 2016, Southwest Florida Pride, Inc. created The Goldberg Award to "recognize outstanding individuals that have contributed to the cultural, social and economic fabric of the LGBTQ+ Community in Southwest Florida. It shall be awarded to the person who in the preceding year has displayed exemplary activity within the LGBTQ+ community. The Goldberg Award seeks to honor the absolute highest levels of achievement of a notable member of the SWFL community."

The author lives by the motto that, "You never know what's going to happen, so I don't waste any time now. I waste no time worrying about things or being angry with people. Nothing is more important than staying in the moment."

She also lives by her God-given intuition. "I always go with my intuition," she explains. "Whatever my heart feels, that's the way I go. I follow my intuition because it is always right. It always takes me in the right direction. My brain on the other hand can lie or steer me wrong. Look at the animals. They always trust their instincts. Without them, they would be dead. It's the same way with me."

"Arlene is a true champion for equality and an inspiration to all. At a time of deep sadness, she refused to sit back and be complacent in the face of discrimination. She moved us all when she stood with pride and unwavering determination and demanded that her marriage to Carol Goldwasser be recognized in Florida. And while she achieved victory for recognition of her own marriage, she continues to stand with pride and unwavering determination to fight for the rights of all same-sex couples in Florida."

~ Nadine Smith, CEO, Equality Florida

"Activist, Leader, Inspiration. Activism may not have been Arlene Goldberg's goal, but her first steps out of the closet and into the growing LGBTQ community in Southwest Florida set her on a path that would not only lead to her marriage being the first same-sex marriage recognized in the state of Florida but cement Arlene's status as a prominent leader and force for change."

~ Grandeur Magazine

"Goldberg successfully fought for her and her late wife, Carol, to become the first legally married same-sex couple in the state of Florida. In making sure that the privileges most of us take for granted are beneficial and fair to all in our community, she lives by the spirit of the 4-Way Test that is our founding principle."

~ The Rotary Club of Fort Myers South

"Arlene Goldberg is a woman of commendable character. Her strength, knowledge and courage are not only an inspiration, but demonstrate the unwavering ability to stand, in the face of adversity, and fight for equality in some of the most basic of human rights. At the 2016 Pride event, Pride-SWFL excitedly unveiled its newest endeavor, the Goldberg Award. The award was inspired by its namesake, Arlene.

She was the first recipient of the award and is one of SWFL's most influentially compassionate members of the LGBTQ community."

~ Southwest Florida Pride

Made in the USA
Columbia, SC
04 December 2020